A Treasury
of
Musical Humor

D1027375

**Edited by
James E. Myers, Sr.**

The Lincoln-Herndon Press, Inc.
818 South Dirksen Parkway
Springfield, Illinois 62703

A Treasury of Musical Humor

Copyright © 1998 by The Lincoln-Herndon Press, Inc.
All rights reserved. This book, or parts thereof, may not be repro-
duced in any form without permission.

Published by

The Lincoln-Herndon Press, Inc.
818 S. Dirksen Parkway
Springfield, Illinois 62703
(217) 522-2732

Printed in the United States of America

LIBRARY OF CONGRESS CATALOGUING-IN-PUBLICATION
DATA

ISBN 0-942936-34-5 $12.95
Library of Congress Catalogue Card Number 98-068114
First Printing

Typography by

Communication Design
Rochester, Illinois

Table of Contents

INTRODUCTION

Most Americans don't think of humor, giggles or laughter when they consider music. But as a matter of fact, Americans and others have been saying funny things — aphorisms, jokes, and cartoons about music for generations. Here are some examples:

- "Classical music is the kind we keep thinking will turn into a tune." Kim Hubbard
- On being asked if Bach was still composing, W.S. Gilbert replied, "No, Madam, he's decomposing."
- "I hate music, especially when it's played." Jimmy Durante
- "Rossini would have been a great composer if his teacher had spanked him sufficiently on the backside." Ludwig Von Beethoven
- "Such a laugh was money in a man's pocket, because it cut down on the doctor's bills like everything." Tom Sawyer
- "Humor is the good-natured side of truth." Interview with Mark Twain

Well, that gives you a brief idea of the timelessness of humor that is related to music.

From these few words the editor invites you to turn to the main body of this book and find humor about opera, symphony, instruments, percussion, winds, voice, 19th Century Humor and a great deal more. If you enjoy the music humor in this book as much as the editor did assembling it, he promises you a delightful and prolonged good time of healthy laughter and added interest in symphony, opera, song, orchestra and instruments, and Jazz.

CHAPTER 1

Strings

Elmer returned from school one day and said, "Hey Mom! In class today I recited the alphabet all the way through but the rest of the class only got up to G."

"That's because you are a violist, Elmer," his mother said.

The next day Elmer came home and said, "Mom! Mom! I counted to 125 today and the rest of the class could only count to 80."

His mother again replied, "That's because you are a violist, Elmer."

The next day Elmer came from school, burst into the house and said, "Momma, Momma, I'm taller than all the others in the class. Is that because I'm a violist?"

"No, dear, that's because you're 25!"

A violinist was asked to write something brief in an autograph album and wasn't just certain what to do. He therefore turned to a fellow musician for advice. The other musician advised him "Just write down your repertoire."

"I practiced three hours on my guitar," said the folk singer pluckily.

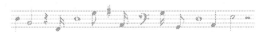

Did you hear about the guy who was so cheap that he made his children take violin lessons so that he wouldn't have to get them haircuts?

Q: What's the best way to keep your violin from being stolen?
   A: Put it in a viola case.

Q: Why was the cellist so very angry at the conductor?
   A: Because he told him to quit scratching that thing between his legs.

Violinist: A musician up to his chin in music.

Tell that violinist who plays out of tune he should play out of town.

Just before one of Mischa Elman's violin recitals, a man burst into his dressing room and greeted him effusively. "We're related, Mr. Elman," he announced. "Your wife's aunt is married to the uncle of my ex-wife's first husband's present wife." Mr. Elman puzzled over this for a moment and then smiled with relief. "It's not so close," he decided, "that I have to give you a free ticket to the concert this evening."

Perhaps it was because Nero played the fiddle that they burned Rome.

Oliver Herford (1863-1935)

John Rosenfeld tells about the lady musician who was fired in disgrace from a nationally famous orchestra. "We had a concert date in Dallas," she explained tearfully, "and I forgot my harp."

Jack Benny told of a day in his youth when he was practicing violin in old Waukegan, Illinois. A dog stood outside the window howling his head off. Benny's father stuck his head inside the door and begged, "For gosh sake, Jack, play something that dog doesn't know!"

Marriage usually brings music into a man's life. He learns to play second fiddle at home.

Schoenberg's *Violin Concerto* combines the best sound effects of a hen yard at feeding time, a brisk morning in Chinatown and practice hour at a busy music conservatory. The impression on the vast majority of hearers is that of a lecture on the fourth dimension delivered in Chinese.

Edwin H. Schloss in the *Philadelphia Record*
December 7, 1940

Violinists: The way some play makes one think the strings are still on the cat.

Jascha Heifetz and Mischa Elman were eating together at a restaurant patronized by many artists. The waiter came to the table and handed them an envelope addressed to "The World's Greatest Violinist."

Heifetz took it from the tray and presented it to Elman, saying, "For you, Mischa." Elman read the outside and said, "No, Jascha, it's for you," and handed it back to him. This went on, back and forth, for some time, until they finally opened it and saw that the letter was addressed, "Dear Fritz."

Love is not the dying moan of a distant violin — it's the triumphant twang of a bedspring.

S. J. Perelman (1904-1979)

A wandering musician was stranded in a small town on Sunday morn. So to make a few pennies he took out his violin, put his hat beside him and began to play for alms.

"I tell you, that guy can get more out of a guitar than anyone in town!"

A minister came walking by and stopped to ask, "Do you know the Fourth Commandment, my good man?"

The musician replied, "I'm not sure I do, but if you'll whistle or hum a few bars of it, I'll try to play it for you."

Playing the violin must be like making love — all or nothing.

Isaac Stern

Whitey Mitchell: Most people cannot resist the temptation to comment humorously on the plight of the bass player carrying his bass to or from work. Each person seems to think that his is a highly original and amusing remark, but any bass player can tell you that all of these hilarious observations derive from a single, ancient chestnut, to wit: "Why didn't you take up the piccolo?"

My brother, Red Mitchell, says there are four cliches normally addressed to bass players. They run approximately as follows:

"What have you got in there, your grandmother?"

"How on earth do you get that thing under your chin?"

"Isn't that an awful big load for a little fellow like you?" (You can be 6' 4" and they'll still throw this line at you.)

"What kind of vitamin pills have you been feeding that fiddle?"

There are, however, a few original souls left in the world, and there is a woman in California eminently qualified to be included in this category. She spotted Red struggling to get to a record date with the bass and immediately invoked: "Well, when you get where you're going, I certainly hope they ask you to play."

"He can always switch to comedy."

Reprinted with permission of
The Saturday Evening Post Society

After his performance in a small town, the violinist was angry when he read the review in the local newspaper. He went to the editor and complained, saying: "I told your reporter that I was playing on a genuine Stradivarius violin, and he never so much as mentioned it in the review."

"He was just following orders," said the editor. "If we advertise any product in our newspaper, it has got to be paid for at one buck a line!"

A rich man was giving a reception at his home and had engaged a violinist to play during the time. The violinist informed him, "I just want you to know, Sir, that my violin is over 200 years old."

"The important thing is to play it well," responded the host. "We'll just dim the lights and nobody will notice it."

"They say she attained her present prominence by pulling wires."

"Really?"

"Yes. She plays the harp."

The wisest gift for a violinist living upstairs is a gift of a violin with no strings attached.

Dan: "Did you hear that Brown made $100.00 playing the violin?"

Nan: "Imagine! 25 bucks a string!"

Dan: "Yeah, he shoulda played a harp!"

Violinist: "The business manager kept calling me to rehearse, but I didn't like what he called me!"

When he was a little boy, Jascha Heifetz was visiting a friend of my family and the host invited him to play something for the assembled people in the parlor. He agreed and played Beethoven's *Kreutzer Sonata* and did well with it. But, as you know, there are a good many long and impressive rests in the piece; and during one of them, an elderly man leaned forward and patted his shoulder and said: "Listen to me, sonny, why don't you play something you know?"

In Chicago a beggar was playing violin outside
Symphony Hall when a little old lady came past and put a
dollar in his cup. She asked him: "Tell me, Sir, did you ever
play inside the hall here?"

"Sure did, Lady," the bum replied. "But I came out here
because I can make lots more money here than in there."

Ukelele: The missing link between music and plain
noise.

After Carl Sandburg had played his guitar for a TV show
recently, the director apologized for all the sneezing and
coughing that had been done by the audience. "They didn't
do it on purpose," said Sandburg indulgently. "They're like
the little boy who sneezed in church, and was reprimanded
by his mother. The boy explained, 'I didn't sneeze the
sneeze, mama; the sneeze sneezed me.'"

Samuel Johnson remarked to a friend during a violin
concert: "Difficult music, you call it, Sir? I wish it were
impossible."

Q: How do you account for bass players having pea-
sized brains?
A: It is caused by alcohol and the resultant swelling.

9

Nut: The slim ridge across the neck of an instrument, such as the violin, near the pegbox. Today the term has come to be applied to those who play the instrument.

"Thanks, Pop!"

Viola: A poor relative to a violin-akin to a ne'er-do-well relative.

The famous violinist had just played at the funeral of the father of a friend. The friend thanked him and asked if he wouldn't play at the friend's funeral too.

"Of course. Just tell me what you'd like to hear," was the reply.

Violin: A bad hotel!

It is said of violinists that they are the only musicians who are "up to their necks in music."

A famous violinist was invited by a Manhattan lady to play at her house for a private party she was giving. He agreed to do it and she asked his fee.

"Three-thousand dollars, Madam," he informed her.

"That's extremely high," she replied, "But I'll pay it. However, you must remember not to mingle with my guest while in my home."

"Madam," the violinist replied, "In that case, I'll play for $1,000!"

At her party, the hostess was asking her guests if they played a musical instrument. If they responded, she asked each to play.

One fellow responded that he did play an instrument, but only at home.

When asked what instrument he played, he replied, "Second fiddle."

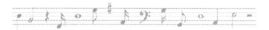

Q: What is an important purpose of a violin?
A: It allows the player to fiddle around.

"In respect to violins, I am polygamous."

Fritz Kreisler

Violin: A gift with strings attached.

Mrs. Van Smarts gave a musicale, presenting a famous violinist. When it was over, everyone applauded and crowded around the musician. Well, almost everyone except one old guy who said, "That was the worst violin playing I've ever heard. It stank to high heaven!"

"Don't listen to that jerk," Mrs. Van Smarts assured the violinist, "He never had an original thought in all of his life. He just repeats what he hears others saying!"

Q: What's the difference between a viola and a steam engine?
A: The intensity of vibrations.

"Looks like Hooper is not getting the raise."

When mother made up her mind that little Bobby was
sure to become a great violinist, Daddy's complaints about
the noise and the expense fell on deaf ears. Finally,
because the music teacher recommended it, he bought
Nathan one of those violins specially designed for kids.

To the surprise of everybody but Mama, Bobby's teacher
demanded that he have a full-sized instrument the very next
year.

Papa lugged himself to the music store, where his eye
fell on a big violoncello. That's the one I'll take," he
announced, smiling. "Let the little dickens learn to outgrow
that!"

Q: What method is used to get a guitar player to play softer?
A: Place a sheet of music in front of him.

Little boy at a cello concert: "Mama, will the concert be over when this guy finishes sawing through the box?"

Please define the word "violin."
That's easy! It's an instrument used by musicians to fiddle around.

During the reception that always followed his concerts, a violinist was asked, "Sir, are you married?"
"Yes, Ma'am, I am."
"And do you have children?"
"Yes, Ma'am, three — two of whom are twins."
"Oh my goodness. Wonderful. But tell us how you felt when you were notified that you were the father of twins?"
"Madam, I felt as if I'd received two fees for one performance."

Walking down the street one day, Fritz Kreisler passed a large fish shop and saw in the window a row of fishes staring out at passersby. The fish had their mouths open, as were their eyes, and lay in a row staring out.
"That reminds me," moaned Kreisler, "I should be playing at my concert."

The violinist Ysaÿe once performed a recital tour through Sweden. Among the pieces was the Bach *Chaconne*. In a small town near Uppsala, he looked through the curtain and saw that his audience seemed to be mainly hicks — farmers in overalls — so he decided that the *Chaconne* would be wasted on them and he played something lighter. After the concert a farmer entered the dressing room and said:

"Mr. Ysaÿe, I traveled fifty kilometers in my horse and cart just to hear you, and you didn't play the *Chaconne*."

Ysaÿe replied, "My dear man, I had no idea that anyone here would either know or give a damn whether I played the *Chaconne* or not. Come back with me to my hotel, we'll have dinner and afterward I shall give you a private concert."

They went back and after dinner enjoyed a liqueur and a good cigar. Ysaÿe then got up, took out his Amati violin and played the *Chaconne*. When he finished, the farmer said:

"Well, well, well, so that's the *Chaconne*. You know, Mr. Ysaÿe, that's the first time I ever heard it. I don't like it."

A stringless violin was displayed in the window of a secondhand store in Chicago with this sign: "This is yours for $35 — no strings attached."

Q: Why are orchestra intermissions held for only twenty minutes?

A: That's so that they won't have to retrain the cellists.

Stringendo: The definition of a destroyed violin or cello.

)1988 North America Syndicate, Inc. All rights reserved.

"It's his annual request for leaner hamburger – set to music."

Americans are so ridden with time-payments that the first thing they do when they get to heaven is to ask if there's a down payment for the harp.

The sweetest music to my girl's ear is another girl playing the second fiddle.

It is well to remember that learning to play the harp is no guarantee that you'll get into heaven.

Q: What do you call five viola players at the bottom of the lake?

A: One heluva good idea!

Cellist #1: "Where do you live?"
Cellist #2: "Just outside of my income."

A famous young violinist was giving a recital at the home of one of New York City's most famous dowagers. He was playing a number that had several long — very long — rests in it. After pausing for several of these rests, he heard the dowager whisper: "Just take it easy, my boy. Don't get upset. Just play something you know really well and we'll all understand."

A man who plays the viola is sometimes called a violator.

"I make forty dollars a night playing the violin. That's ten dollars a string."
"Aren't you sorry you didn't learn to play the harp?"

Backstage Manager: "He knows everything about music."
Errand Boy: "Oh, not everything."

17

Manager: "What is there about music that he doesn't know?"

Errand Boy: "That I just dropped his violin down the elevator shaft."

"Have you a zither?"

"No, but I've got a couple of brothers."

Desk clerk at hotel: "Sir, did you have a chance to practice your violin in your room?"

"Sure did! I practiced there this morning."

"Oh my gosh! I thought...I thought well, I had the janitor oil the door hinges to your door."

Rubinoff, famed musician of an earlier time, told this story:

After finishing my regular concert I addressed the audience and asked them to write any request they had on a piece of paper and I'd play it. Only one piece came forward and it read, "Play good."

"How do you think Jake is progressing as a violinist?"

"I think he's got a long way to go before he's a concert musician."

"Really? How did you come to that conclusion?"

"Well the other day I was accompanying him and my piano got up and walked out."

To be distinctly successful, a cellist must have distinctly bowed legs.

The music teacher wanted to impress the class with the dignity of musical instruments, so she started with strings: "Do you realize, class, that the guitar is over two thousand years old?"

"Impossible," replied one student. "Why they didn't even have electricity back then!"

Most string quartets have a basement and an attic, but the elevator is not working.

Neville Cardus
The Delights of Music (1966)

My girl is so thin she could walk through a harp without hitting a string. And, what's more, she could tap dance on a chocolate eclair.

There is a lovely saying about marriage as music: "Marriage is like a violin." Now, isn't that sweet and gentle? Then it goes on to say: "Yes, but after the beautiful music is over, the strings are still attached!"

The audience strummed their cattarhs.

Alexander Woollcott
(1887-1943)

"I said no doggie tricks 'til after dinner."

"It got to the point where I had to get a haircut or a violin."

Franklin D. Roosevelt
(1882-1945)

Q: Why is it that cello players rarely catch cold?
A: Because even viruses have their share of pride.

"Maestro, I hope you'll excuse my performance of that piece. I haven't played the violin in almost a year."
"What year?"

Elmer Shadduck was the town's old curmudgeon and vociferous critic of everybody and everything. When he was informed that his neighbor Paul Tillitt owned a 200-year-old violin, he remarked: "Beats the hell out of me why that old geezer don't throw away that old fiddle and buy him a new one. Lord knows he can afford it!"

Q: How do you get a violinist away from your front door?
A: Pay for the pizza!

A certain violinist was convinced that his music could make docile any creature. So he took himself and his instrument to a village of monsters and began to play his instrument in the most beautiful and touching manner. The monsters began to gather around him, and it was obvious that they were thrilled, utterly delighted. Then, without warning, one of them approached the rear of the violinist and threw a spear through his heart.

"You fool! Why did you do that?" the crowd cried, "We loved his music!"

The murderer cupped his hand behind his ear and asked, "Eh?"

The ukelele is a so-called musical instrument which, when listened to, you cannot tell whether someone is playing it or just monkeying with it.

Will Rogers
(1876-1935)

"How much do you think I earned on my last concert tour? " a famous violinist asked of a competitive concert violinist.

"I'd guess about half," was the reply.

Q: Why did the chicken cross the road?
A: It wanted to avoid the violin solo.

America's most famous and talented string quartet was performing in Columbus, Ohio. During the intermission, a sweet old gentleman remarked to the director, "It's just too bad that you can't afford a full orchestra and have to make-do with only four players."

One of my jobs with the British army in Egypt was to organize concerts. This meant not only getting players and singers together but also finding someone to type out the programs.

On one occasion we had scheduled a violinist and pianist to play Handel's *Sonata in A Major*. The orderly-room clerk got the particulars right, but he gave them an unusually military spacing:

> Ian Parrott (Aberystwyth, Wales)
> Handel's *Sonata in A...Major*

Gentleman: A fellow who *could* play the banjo but doesn't.

Perhaps the briefest of reviews ever appeared in the
New York Times. It read: "The string quartet played several
tunes by Brahms. Brahms lost!"

Although his comfortable home was at the base of the
mountain, why did the violinist insist on going to the side of
the mountain every day to practice?
Because he was musically inclined.

At the pop concert the conductor demanded that all
banjo players all wear special trousers. What kind were
they? CORD-u-roys, of course!

Q: Why are harps like one's elderly parents?
A: They're both hard to get out of a car.

"You were formerly one of my regular attenders at
Sunday church. But now, I don't ever see you in church.
Why?"
"Well, parson, I'll tell you. My daughter is now taking
harp lessons and I'm not sure now that I want to go to
heaven."

The symphony orchestra was being entertained by its
Board of Directors at a dinner. During dessert, a board
member asked the first violinist, "Tell me, Mr. Murdoch, do
you practice your violin at home?"

"Oh yes," he replied, "But not like at orchestra hall. At home I play second fiddle."

What is the dessert preferred by orchestral string instrument sections?
Cello.

If a theatrical play were written that described a violinist on a ten-mile hike, what would the title be?
FIDDLER ON THE HOOF, of course!

Q: What is the best instrument to accompany a banjo?
A: A chain saw.

What this country needs is more folk singers who can carry a tune and fewer who carry a guitar.

There was once a violinist with a beard so thick that he had to kiss his wife through a straw.

My violin lessons with my neighbor, Mr. Edwards, cost ten dollars. One day another neighbor offered me fifteen dollars an hour to give it up. Still another neighbor offered me twenty bucks an hour if I'd destroy my violin. This last offer was from Mr. Edwards.

GC PSTEIN

"Before beginning my excuse, Mr. Zabelli here will play a short, romantic selection."

Reprinted with permission of
The Saturday Evening Post Society

The Man from Vermont and the Bass Viol

Now there was this man from Vermont. I should tell you
that I used to tell this story and I'd say, "There was a man
from Delaware" and everybody would look back and
everything would always go flat. Then I just happened to
say, "A man from Vermont" one time and the whole hall just
laughed their heads off. I don't have to be hit in the head

with a hammer to get a message. So ever since then, it's been a man from Vermont.

This man from Vermont, he was a pokey old cuss. When his wife was all through eating, for example, he'd still be picking away at his plate. When his wife was all washed up, he'd still be settin' there.

One day, though, he went to an auction and he picked up a bass viol. He brought it home and it just transformed him. Every night he'd bolt his supper down just as fast as he could and he'd get in the Sittin' Room and he'd get that thing out and get it down between his legs and tighten the bow and he'd start, just playing the same note. And he'd play that same note again and again. That went on for weeks. His wife was patient, figuring he'd move on to another note soon or later. One night, she finally broke down and she said, "Ethan?"

"Yup?"

"Did you ever hear anyone play a bass viol?"

"Lots of people."

She said, "Didn't you notice they run their fingers up and down?"

He said, "Yes. But they were still looking for their place. I found mine!"

"My grandson just left for Europe to study violin."
"Why Europe?"
"The neighbors insisted."

Q: How many bass players does it take to change a light bulb?

A: None! They are so very macho that they'd as soon walk in the dark and stub their toes on tables and chairs.

CHAPTER 2

Keyboard

When a piece gets difficult, make faces.
                    Arthur Schnabel to Vladimir Horowitz

Chopin was a truly celebrated pianist and, one time in Paris, he was invited to perform at a private party. He played only one short number and prepared to depart. The anxious hostess cried, "Is that all you're going to play?"

"But madam," replied Chopin, "I ate so little."

"I must tell you that my daughter's home piano lessons and daily practice have made a fortune for me."

"Really! I've never heard of such a thing."

"Yep! It's true. Her music enabled me to buy the neighbors' houses at just about half-price."

"They tell me that you love music."

"I sure do, but just keep on playing your piano anyway."

Paderewski once admitted that he practiced every single day! "If I miss one day," he explained, "I notice it. If I miss two days, the critics notice it. And if I miss three days, the audience notices it."

Sound: A condition of mental mind-set hardly ever obtained by pianists.

A piano student needed a certain piece of piano music and hurried down to the local music store to buy it. But the door was closed with a sign on it that read: "Johann to lunch. Bach at one. Offenbach sooner."

Will Rogers, America's favorite laconic philosopher, was once asked to endorse a particular piano. But he never endorsed any product — as a matter of policy. He made an exception in this case, however, saying: "Dear Sirs, I guess your pianos are the best I ever leaned against." Yours Truly, Will Rogers.

The music teacher came twice a week to bridge the awful gap between Dorothy and Chopin.

                                        Kim Hubbard (1868-1936)

Asked to describe a pianoforte, Leigh Hunt (1784-1859) remarked: "A pianoforte is a harp in a box."

One concert pianist was describing the technique of a rival pianist. "That ivory smacker is just something special — he conquers the simplest, easiest passages with absolutely the utmost difficulty."

"If you ask me, that's the way Prelude in C Sharp Minor should be played."

Reprinted with permission of
The Saturday Evening Post Society

The late C. C. Spaulding of Durham was president of the North Carolina Insurance Company, the largest Negro insurance company in the world. A mighty fine man from every point of view.

A year or so before his death, Mr. Spaulding appeared before a legislative committee in Raleigh and made a talk about the proposed hospitalization program. He said the members of his race were heartily in favor of this program and he urged the members of the committee to vote for it. Adding that it would be of great benefit to Negroes throughout North Carolina, he would up by saying: "You know, you can't very well play 'The Star Spangled Banner' on the piano without making use of the black keys occasionally."

Carl Goerch
Just for the Fun of It (1954)

Bob: "My brother plays the piano by ear."
Tom: "So what? My granddaddy fiddles with his whiskers."

A young lady asked Rubinstein, the superb pianist, to hear her play the piano. He agreed and she played for him. Afterwards, she asked, "What do you think I should do now, Maestro?"
"Get married!" was his reply.

Then up rose Ignatius Paderewski,
And said, "I don't know what to doski
　　when I go out for air
　　the wind gets in my hair
And it looks just as though I were Blewski."

Jascha Heifetz once spent a summer vacation in Lake Placid, in the Adirondacks. The lady in the cottage next door practiced piano regularly for an hour each morning, Heifetz or no Heifetz. What's more, she played terribly.
One day a stranger appeared at her door and said, "I'm the piano tuner." "I didn't order any piano tuner," expostulated the lady. "You didn't," agreed the piano tuner, "but Mr. Heifetz did."

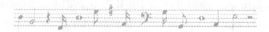

He was as unlucky in death as in life. When he went to heaven they gave him an unlisted harp!

Arthur Rubinstein, in order to practice for a concert, told his butler, Francois, to tell any callers that he was not at home. When the telephone rang, a woman's voice asked for the maestro. With the crashing chords of Rubinstein's rehearsal thundering in from the next room, the butler suavely informed the woman his master was out. "Out?" she protested. "But I can hear him playing!"

"Not at all, Madam," the resourceful Francois told her imperturbably. "It is merely I, dusting the keys."

A person who tells you he loves bagpipe music will lie about other things too.

"Madam, I've come to tune your piano."
"But I didn't send for a piano-tuner."
"I know that, Lady. Your neighbors did."

During World War II, a musician was drafted and went before the draft board. "I'm a musician," he complained, "I'd be of no use in the service!"

"You're mistaken," the head of the draft board said. "You'll inspire the soldiers on to great deeds with your music. Just imagine yourself in the trenches with the infantry, waiting to go over the top, inspiring your fellow buddies to fight even harder with your music. By the way, what do you play?"

"I play piano," moaned the draftee.

Drawings by Booth © 1976
The New Yorker Magazine, Inc.

It's reported that there is not a single pipe organ in heaven. Why? Probably because they needed the keys in hell to make accordions.

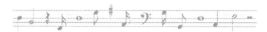

At the finish of one of his superb concerts, the great pianist Sergei Rachmaninoff was asked: "What superb, sublime thoughts were going through your musical head as the orchestra played your beautiful music?"

Rachmaninoff replied: "I was counting the house, the attendance."

Out of the past comes a great story about two old men walking along the street in the Bronx when the chimes of a nearby cathedral floated through the air. One old man said: "Isn't that lovely music?"

The second man said, "Eh?"

So the first fellow repeated more loudly: "Isn't that lovely music?"

"I give up!" was the other old boy's reply. "Those golderned bells are making so derned much noise that I can't hear what you're saying!"

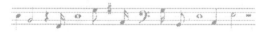

He has always been musical. As a child he played on the floor but now he plays on the piano.

Fred: "You think your son plays the piano like Paderewski?"

Ted: "Yep. He uses both hands."

He was a piano mover but not very good at his trade because he couldn't carry a tune.

My gal is really strong — big and strong," said one guy to his friend. "She works in a piano factory and is the official piano mover. She weighs 300 pounds and I call her my oomph girl."
"Why do you call her that?" his friend asked.
"Because every time she sits on the sofa it goes 'oomph!'"

"I do most of my work sitting down," said the piano player. "That's where I shine!"

At an important concert, one selection required sixteen pianos and pianists, all on stage together. The conductor, Moritz Moszkowski, turned to the audience and remarked: "What they need here is a traffic cop, not a conductor!"

Hostess: "They all tell me you love music."
Guest: "Yep! Sure do. But don't let that bother you…keep right on playing."

Visitor: "Tell me…does your son play on the piano?"
Mother: "No. He can't climb that high."

The piano is a musical utensil for subduing the impenitent visitor. It is operated by depressing the keys of the machine and the spirits of the audience.

Ambrose Bierce
(1842-1914)

Polite Visitor: "Your Bobby is making great progress with his piano since I heard him last. He is beginning to play quite well."

Bobby's Mother: "Oh, do you really think so? His daddy and I wonder if we'd merely gotten used to it."

Did you hear the story about the pretty blonde who told the amorous piano player to keep his dissonance?

Time after time, concerts and plays at the City Auditorium have been interrupted by tardy ones traipsing down the aisle. A very bad one was a local dowager who was always late. She obviously enjoyed every minute of her march to her first row seat.

Oscar Levant was in the middle of a number one evening when this socialite and her entourage arrived. She was resplendent in jewels and furs — and all eyes turned to watch the entrance. As she came down the aisle, the pianist stopped his performance of a Beethoven concerto and began to mimic her walk by playing in time with her steps. She slowed down — Levant slowed down. She stopped — Levant stopped. She hurried — Levant hurried. By the time she reached her seat, the audience was in hysterics and the show-off was in a state of wild confusion.

The next time there was a performance at the auditorium, she arrived a good fifteen minutes before curtain time and at all succeeding performances!

A New York lady, famous for her social soirees, invited a crusty old hermit to hear a famous pianist. After several pieces were performed on her Steinway Grand piano, the lady walked up to the hermit and asked: "Are you enjoying yourself, Sir?"

"I sure am, ma'am — and that's all I'm enjoying!"

Q: Why did the organist refuse to allow girls to sing?
A: Because she wanted a hymn.

An organ grinder was playing and begging just outside Verdi's window. The composer stuck his head out the window and told the organist that he was playing much too loud. The next day the organist appeared carrying his instrument and a sign reading: "VERDI'S PUPIL."

You can't beat an American when it comes to bargaining. Consider this budding American pianist following his concert in Germany. The M.C. asked him if he'd prefer a decoration or 100 marks.

"Well that depends," the American asked, "How much is the decoration worth?"

"About twenty marks," was the reply.

"Ok, then, just give me the decoration and 80 marks."

A famous pianist cut a dangerous rug with his pupils, especially the girls. Once while giving a lesson to a banker's daughter in the banker's home, he had just put his arm around the girl and was about to kiss her when the father appeared.

"Is this what I'm paying you to do?" barked the father.

"Sir, No! I do this for nothing," was the reply.

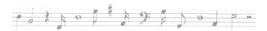

Nothing soothes me more, after a long and maddening course of pianoforte recitals than to sit and have my teeth drilled.

George Bernard Shaw

When only a child, the artist Josef Hofmann had a command performance before the German emperor. Hofmann was only nine years old, but all the other artists were adults. At the conclusion of the concert, the M.C. handed

Hofmann's father 200 franks, but the other artists were handed twice that. When Mr. Hofmann asked why his nine-year-old only got half that paid the adults, he was told: "Children under ten get half fare!"

Famed pianist of an earlier time, Ignace Paderewski, was once asked by a famous polo player: "What's the difference between you and me?"

"That's a simple question to answer," replied Paderewski. "You are a good soul who plays polo, while I am a poor Pole who plays solo."

Q: What key do you get when you drop a baby grand piano down a coal mine shaft?

A: A-flat minor-r-r.

A recent "outer space" story concerns a curious little "other-world" creature who dropped in on Manhattan. The alien walked by a music store that displayed a piano in the window.

"Doggone you," the creature snarled, "Wipe that silly smile off your face!"

Back home, Johnny told his mother that his music teacher Mr. Jones had asked if he had any brothers or sisters who played an instrument. "I said no," the boy replied.

"And what did Mr. Jones say after that?" his mother asked.

"He said, 'Thank goodness!'"

"I donated it to our church."

"Tell me, Mabel, is our friend Jim now a virtuoso?"
"How should I know! I know nothing about his personal life!"

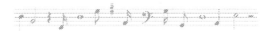

Irving Berlin once urged Victor Borge to stick to the classics.
"But, Irving, every time I play Mozart, I hear a little voice that whispers, 'Don't play it. Don't play it.'"
"You recognize the little voice?"
"Yes, Irving. It's Mozart's."

Sweet Lily's a pianist and
 Causes quite a stir,

'Cause all the musicians are very anxious
To play a rondo with her.

"What skills must I learn to play the accordion?" asked
the customer.

"It's simple," replied the salesman, "Just practice folding
and unfolding a road map."

Mother called on her son's piano teacher to see just how
he was progressing.

She was delighted to hear the teacher say, "In at least
one feature, he plays just like Jose Iturbi —"

"And what is that feature?" the doting mother asked.

"He plays with two hands."

Asked for the secret to his piano virtuosity, the great
artist replied, "I always make sure the lid of the keyboard is
open before I start to play."

Little League baseball was the boy's greatest obsession.
His determined mother, though, insisted that he had to learn
to play the piano and kept him on strict schedule of practice.

"What are you going to be when you grow up?" a visitor
to the house asked him one spring day.

"Well," he replied, "it looks as if I'm going to be the first
concert pianist to play center field for the Yankees."

Music devotee: "I'm so sorry that I can't attend your charity piano concert but you can be sure that I'll be there in spirit."

Ticket salesman: "That's okeedokee, but where would you like your spirit to sit? Tickets sell for five, ten, and fifteen dollars!"

"We've got to get him one of those play pools."

Hughie: "Yes, since you ask — I do play entirely by ear."

Lewie: "Interesting! But just remember — People listen that same way!"

She laughed when I sat down to play. How could I know she was ticklish!

The bill collector for the music store knocked on Findlay's door and said, "I've come to collect the money due on the piano you got from our store."

The householder replied, "But your company advertises that 'You pay as you play,' doesn't it?"

"That's true, but that has nothing to do with the money you owe us."

"It certainly does — I play poorly."

Joe Anderson went into a bar and after he had a couple of drinks he said to the bartender, "Do you want to see something amazing?"

The bartender said, "Sure."

So Joe took out a tiny piano and a stool and he laid them on the bar.

The bartender said, "That's cute."

Then Joe said, "Wait, wait, you haven't seen anything yet." And he reached into his vest pocket and he took out a tiny mouse and he sat the mouse down on the stool and said, "Play." And the mouse started to beat out Rachmaninoff and Bach and Brahms and Beethoven.

The bartender said, "That's marvelous! I've never seen anything like it before."

And everyone in the bar started to come up and watch.

Joe said, "Aw, you haven't seen anything yet."

And he pulled out another little mouse and he put it next to the piano and said, "Sing." And while the pianist mouse was beating out the rhythm, the singing mouse sang arias from *La Traviata* and from *Tristan and Isolde.* Everybody in the bar was just thunderstruck.

One fellow said, "That's the most wonderful thing I've seen in my life. I'll give you twenty thousand dollars for that. Cash on the spot."

The bartender said, "Don't sell, Joe. That thing's worth a million dollars on television."

Joe replied, "Aw, I've got to sell them. I need the money."

So Joe took the twenty thousand dollars and the other fellow took the two mice and the piano and walked out.

The bartender said, "Boy! Are you crazy! You could have made a fortune with that."

"Aw, don't be silly! It's a phony!"

"What do you mean a phony?"

"That mouse can't sing!" Joe said. "The one at the piano is a ventriloquist!"

Adcox Associates, Inc.

"You didn't!!"

A famous concert pianist was annoyed at finding that his piano stool was not high enough. He asked for a telephone directory to give added height, got it, put it atop the stool, sat, then shook his head because it was still too low. So he tore off one sheet, laid it on the stool, once again sat down and, low and behold, he smiled in utter delight and began playing.

A certain young lady named Hannah,
Was caught in a flood in Montana
    As she floated away,

44

Her beau, so they say,
Accompanied her on the piannah.

Pianist: "They tell me that you are a lover of fine music. Is that true?"

Patron: "Oh, yes. But don't let that bother you. Just keep on playing!"

The famous pianist had just finished his recital in a small midwestern town, and tea was being served by the local music society. A woman snuggled up to the pianist and asked for advice.

"Sir, I just loved that last piece you played and I need to know what it was so I can buy it for my daughter so's she can learn it."

"Madam, the music you liked was a piano work by Schumann, *Opus 23, Number 4*."

"Oh, that's just swell," she gushed. "Because I do so love Opuses!"

Little Sally was practicing piano when she hit a really foul chord and immediately exclaimed, "Pregnant!"

"Why did you use that word?" her shocked mother asked.

"Because last night I heard you tell Daddy you were pregnant and Daddy said: "That's a hell of a note!"

"When I completed my concert at Carnegie Hall, the entire audience rose as one man and applauded!"

"Yeah, I heard about that. You marched right down in front and shook hands with him."

Head of the music department to an untalented student: "You should go a long way — and the sooner the better!"

The town gossip finally got into the home of a leading citizen. And, after leaving, soon spread this news: "He ain't doin' so well, from the looks of things. I seen his two daughters sittin' together playing on ONE piano."

"Fom the top – 'Watermelon Man.' Let's sock it out and give Mrs. Ritterhouse a chance to really cook!"

Drawing by Booth © 1976
The New Yorker Magazine, Inc.

Here's a witty Vermont story: In the mid-1940s, Harry S. Truman, who wasn't a great hero to Vermont folks naturally, became the butt of many stories. Shortly after Truman assumed the presidency, a Vermonter was asked what he thought of him.

"Don't think much of him," was the answer. "Fact is, he reminds me a great deal of my uncle's piano."

"What do you mean by that?" he was asked.

"Well now, that's right. I guess you didn't know my Uncle Charlie. He was a sort of black sheep of the family and not over-bright. Years ago, he went down to Philadelphia, got a job down there playing piano in a house of ill-repute. And y'know what — he played that piano for two years before he had the faintest idea what was going on upstairs.

— From *What the Old Timer and Then Some Said to the Feller From Down Country*

by Allen R. Foley
Brattleboro, VT:
Stephen Green Press

They laughed when he sat down to play the piano. And y'know what — they're *still* laughing.

"My wife aspired to become a concert pianist but now that the baby has come she doesn't practice anymore."

"My, children can be a comfort, can't they?"

Q: Why is a concert grand piano better than a studio upright?

A: Because it makes a simply sensational "kerblam" when you drop it over a cliff.

A woman in line was surprised to see the piano player ahead of her. She asked him "Are you always nervous before you play?"

"No, not especially so," he replied, "Why do you ask?"

"Because you're standing in the line for the ladies room!"

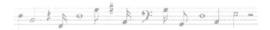

"I hear that you had a falling-out with your neighbor."

"Yep! As you know, my three kids are all taking piano lessons and they love it and practice a lot. Well, the other day the guy next door sent us an axe with a note saying: 'Here's something for your kids to try out on your piano.'"

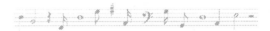

"I'm sure sorry, Dear," the wife said as the music store truckers came upstairs and began to repossess the piano.

"But I gave you the money to make the payments!" hubby shouted.

"I know, I know," his wife replied. "And as soon as they get downstairs I'll pay 'em. It's just that I don't like the piano on the second floor. Can you think of a better, easier way to move it downstairs than this?"

There was a revival meeting at a church in the deep south and everybody who was important in the community was attending. The preacher had finished his sermon and now turned to his hymn book. "Brothers and Sisters — let us now turn to Hymn 24."

The organist turned to the preacher and said, "But Brother Preacher, I don't know that one."

The preacher turned to the congregation again, saying, "Now Brothers and Sisters, turn to page twelve.

But, the organist said, "I don't know Number 12."

So, once again, the preacher turned to the congregation and said, "Brothers and Sisters, turn to page 62."

Once again, the organist shook his head. From the back
of the hall came the yell, "Throw the sonovabitch out!"

The preacher was appalled, absolutely speechless.
Finally he swallowed and yelled, "Hear me now, Brothers
and Sisters, we cannot allow that kind of profanity in the
house of our Lord! I demand that the person who called our
organist a 'son of a bitch' stand and confess before the congregation!" Not a person rose. The preacher once again
said, "Then I want the person who sits next to the person
who called Brother Organist a sonovabitch, to stand." Not a
soul moved! At the end of his patience, the preacher shouted, "Will the person who sits next to the person who sits
next to the man who uttered that profanity stand!"

Presently a voice in the back of the hall called, "Hey
y'all," then hemmed and hawed as he stood and announced,
"Now, Brother Preacher — I'm not the sonovabitch who
called our brother organist a sonovabitch, but what I want to
know is—who's the sonovabitch that called him an organ
player?"

GEORGE
CRENSHAW

© Field Enterprises, Inc., 1983

"We've got to get him a harp!"

An ambitious mother persuaded the great pianist Arthur Rubinstein to listen to her twelve-year-old son massacre a nocturne by Chopin. At the conclusion of the demonstration, Rubinstein announced, "Madam, without question that is the worst piano playing I have ever heard." Whereupon the mother nodded happily and said to her son, "You see? Now will you give up those expensive piano lessons and go out for soccer?"

Shy Dave, when he attended a party, always chose to sit on the piano bench. He was asked why he sat on the bench but never played the piano. He replied: "I don't play because I don't know how. But this way, sitting here, I keep others from playing it."

Basketball was the boy's greatest obsession. His determined mother, though, insisted that he had to learn to play the piano and kept him on a strict schedule of practice.

"What are you going to be when you grow up?" a visitor to the house asked him one spring day.

"Well," he replied, "It looks as if I'm going to be the first concert pianist in the NBA."

There once was a Happy Hyena
Who played on an old concertina
   He dressed very well
   And in his lapel
He carelessly stuck a verbena.

"Do you play the piano a lot?" the man asked of his date at her house.

"Not so much," she replied. "Only to kill time."

"Well, I must say that you've got a great weapon for that."

"Hey Johnny! Where's your kid brother?"

"He's in the house. We was playing a duet — but I finished first."

A self-made millionaire whose only interest was money asked a famed pianist to his home to play during a party. The musician accepted because of the large sum the man was willing to pay. The pianist performed beautifully, and after one great selection, the host asked, "And who was the composer of that lovely number?"

"Beethoven," was the reply.

"And is he still composing?" the culture-starved host asked.

"No," was the reply, "He's decomposing."

"I will now play a prelude by Chopin," announced Victor Borge. "The Steinway Company asked me to announce that this is a Baldwin piano!"

When Victor Borge was asked why his piano keys were so yellow, he replied: "It's not that the piano is so old — it's just that the elephant smoked too much."

"Now, Daddy doesn't want to say anything to kill your incentive; however, it is 6 A.M."

Reprinted with permission of
The Saturday Evening Post Society

There was a lady pianist who played the piano but not at all like other pianists. She wore gloves. "Why gloves?" she was asked.

"I want to mute the sound so as not to disturb the neighbors," she replied.

Larry: It'd sure be nice if you'd open the piano."
Curly: "I'd like to, but I can't. The keys are inside!"

That guy hates music so much that he even has a stringless piano in his house.

"Do you enjoy Chopin?"

"Heck no! I'm tired and bored from goin' from store to store."

At Carnegie Hall in New York, a famous pianist took a final bow, then retired, depressed, to his dressing room. He would see nobody. He had given a terrible performance and knew it. "Cheer up," counseled his manager. "We all have our off days. You had one coming to you."

The pianist finally was reconciled, and he and his manager went to a nearby restaurant for refreshments. One of the pianist's bitterest rivals suddenly appeared and cried, "Buddy! You were terrific tonight! Magnificent!"

The pianist turned pale and whispered to his manager, "Hells Bells! Was I *that* awful?"

Q: "What's the most difficult part to render on your piano?"

A: "The installments when due!"

Someone once compared a pianist's fingers to lightning. How do you explain that?

Because, so he claimed, a piano player's fingers rarely strike the same place twice!

Until recently, there existed in the Bowery in New York City an ancient restaurant where Irving Berlin would come and play for a few pennies and even wait on tables, trying to make a living.

Now every guide includes the spot on his itinerary. One night, a guide announced to his patrons that on that very piano Berlin had composed his famous song, "White Christmas."

Then, one evening, Irving Berlin, in a nostalgic mood, made an appearance at his old haunt. He sat at the piano and began to sing and play "Oh, How I Hate to Get Up in the Morning." Halfway through the piece, a busload of tourists came in and their guide began his spiel. "Now folks, that geek over there is playing the same piano that Oiving Boilin used to play on and that song is one of Boilin's own tunes!"

The guide walked over to the piano and yelled, "If Oiving Boilin could hear the way you are moiderin' that number of his, he'd toin over in his grave."

An old story that Liberace the pianist himself told went like this: "When music critics lambast me with a bad review, I feel so hurt that I cry all the way to the bank!"

Accordion: Instrument in harmony with the sentiments of an assassin.

Ambrose Bierce
(1842-1914)

In his description of King's College Chapel, David Wilcox remarked, "It's the building's acoustics that are so wonderful. They'd make a fart sound like a seven-fold Amen."

Musician: Many a pianist who plays Chopin should play bridge.

A bosomy young pianist attracted much attention in the world of musicians with her swinging of the classics. Pianist Arthur Rubinstein went to see her one evening and was very much impressed.

"A great pianist like yourself? Well, I don't imagine you'd be so impressed with her Bach," a friend remarked.

"It isn't her Bach," exclaimed Rubinstein. "It's her front!"

© 1988 North America Syndicate, Inc. All rights reserved.

"Like I've always said, his bach is worse than his bite!"

Organ recital: That about which a patient complains of to his doctor.

Having a baby is like trying to push a grand piano through the transom.

I went to all that trouble just to bring a piano player to Chicago only to learn that he doesn't like music.

George Burns

I'm a concert pianist. That's a pretentious way of saying I'm unemployed at the moment.

Oscar Levant
(1906-1972)

"People take off their hats to me and my accordion playing."

"Oh, are you an accomplished player?"

"No, all I can play is 'The Star Spangled Banner.'"

For a dinner party, the first Mrs. John D. Rockefeller, Jr., asked orchestra leader Meyer Davis to provide a string orchestra with ten violins. Davis scrambled about and got the required men, but at the last moment, one of them became ill. When hurried phone calls failed to produce a substitute, Davis said to a top pianist who always accompanied him on his jobs, "Mrs. Rockefeller wants ten violins — and ten she'll get. Tonight you play the violin!"

"But I can't play the violin!" sputtered the pianist.

"Well, sit there and make like a violinist," said Davis, taking his own fiddle from the case and soaping the bow. What Davis hadn't counted on was that, although no violinist, the musician was a terrific actor. He sat there dreamily drawing his bow back and forth — making not a sound, but looking like a dedicated Heifetz. Before long, Mrs. Rockefeller beckoned to Davis. "That violinist!" she beamed. "He's an artist! Can you ask him to play a solo for us?"

Davis thought fast. "Mrs. Rockefeller," he replied grandly, "He is not only a fine artist, but versatile. Did you know he is an even better pianist?" The piano was rolled out and the "violinist" gave the performance of his life.

© Field Enterprises, Inc., 1975

"If you don't like the tune, just say so!"

Basil Rathbone was visiting in Victor Borge's hotel room, and Borge was describing for him the universality of the piano. He told Rathbone that he could even tell time by the piano. The actor looked skeptical; so Borge sat down and jammed out a few bars from a Sousa march. Immediately, there was a pounding on the wall and a sleepy voice yelled: "Stop that noise, you fool! Don't you know it's two o'clock in the morning?"

"You don't know how to take me," the conductor remarked to the furious musician he had scolded.
"Yes I do," she replied, taking him by the ear!

Talk about rapid progress in music! We knew a fellow who two months ago couldn't carry a tune. Now he's a piano mover.

V is vivacious Viola
   Who plays on an old pianola
My thoughts at this time
Are not fit for rhyme,
But I've verified V for Viola.

CHAPTER 3

Boo Boos and Other Verbal Mishaps

Only tight members were present at the C Sharp Club.

In Spain the catarrh is the most popular instrument.

In *The Band Wagon*, a revolting stage was a most effective novelty.

The prima dona got a huge bone out of a very tiny mouth.

The opera singer advertised for a husband and got ten replies in response. She is still unmarried.

The famous singer, Geraldine Farrar, decided to retire at fifty and give other younger singers a chance to sin.

After her rendition of "Annie Laurie," the Bishop sent her a message.

The Williamsburg choral union offered a scared cantata.

Customer at a music store: "I want a piece by the English composer Elgar."
Clerk: "What is the title, Ma'am?"
Customer: "I think it's called 'Pump and Circumcision!'"

The Steinway is the instrument of the immorals.

Tchaikovsky wrote sex symphonies.

He was admitted into the emergency ward at the hospital, suffering from a painful melody.

"I have music in my very soul!"
"Yes, I thought I heard your shoes squeak."

A four-year-old girl was heard singing "God Bless America" this way: "Stand beside her, and guide her, through the night with a light from a bulb."

A California teacher discovered one of her youngsters singing with great seriousness: "My country 'tis of thee, sweet land of liberty, of thee I sing. Land where my fathers died, land of the pills inside —"

There once was a voice man who was going to write a drinking song, but he was never able to get past the first two bars.

New item in Arizona weekly: "Mrs. John Smith and Mrs. Fred Jones sang a duet: 'The Lord Knows Why.'"

A professor of physics at the University of Illinois was on leave in England for six months of study at Oxford. He went to hear a concert of the famous University Boys' Choir. He was wonderfully impressed, almost overcome with the beauty of the boyish voices and, as he described it later to friends, "It was so beautiful that I was almost overcome. It was truly urethral."

A sign in the Bronx says: "Piano lessons — special pains given to beginners."

The music teacher asked her class: "What is a scale?" One class member replied: "It's a freckle on a fish."

Ghosts dearly love music — especially those haunting tunes.

At the monthly meeting of the Sacred Choral Group, modern music was cussed from every angle.

Some kinds of entertainment have to be sin to be properly appreciated.

New item from Iowa newspaper: "REGULAR WEEKLY BAD CONCERT WEDNESDAY NIGHT."

There was a children's concert in St. Louis and the conductor was explaining jazz to his juvenile audience. "You might say that jazz is an irregular, unsteady and exhilarated movement from bar to bar."

A little boy, about ten years old, whispered a question to his mother: "Mama, isn't that what Daddy calls a binge?"

Name Dracula's favorite song.
"Fangs for the Memory."

Music hath charms to soothe the savage beast, but I'd try a revolver first.

Josh Billings

Malaprops in spades! "There's a dirge of good music on the radio."

And from a small-town Kansas newspaper: "The song fest was hell at the Methodist Church Wednesday."

A small-town Tennessee newspaper: "The all-girl orchestra was rather weak in the bras section."

"The quartet sang an interesting derangement of a contemporary song."

Molly: "Did you know that an overweight ghost haunts our local opera house?"

Sally: "Yep! They named it 'Fat-um of the Opera.'"

One of the first and most important things for a critic to learn is how to sleep undetected at the opera.

William Archer

A good music critic is a man who leaves no turn unstoned.

Bernard Shaw

Show me a critic without prejudice and I'll show you an arrested cretin.

George Jean Nathan

I take no more notice of the wind that comes out of the mouths of critics than of the wind expelled from their backsides.

Leonardo

Most critics act on the principle that a composer is ruined by praise and saved by criticism.

A critic is a man without faults. But the people he writes about are loaded with them.

One Sunday we went to church with our kids and the choir sang, "When the Roll Is Called Up Yonder." Tommy, our four-year-old, began to sing it while on our way home. His version: "When the *Biscuit* Is Called Up Yonder."

A conductor of operas in America had two great sopranos who each weighed over 300 pounds. When he introduced them he would say, "I want you to meet my two splendid prima 'tonas!'"

The national anthem of Canada is "O Canada," and the first line is, "Land of our forebearers."

The teacher of a class in history asked if anyone would define "forebear," and one lad stood and said, "Black, brown, polar and grizzly."

A child wrote about his life at home in a school essay. One sentence read: "My sister plays the violin after school, but only for her own amazement."

The editor of the paper thought the sentence too gross and ordered the offensive word "navel" removed. The next day, the editor was far more upset when he read the corrected sentence: "The clarinet player spent the evening staring at his —."

There was an old crow
  who sat upon a clod;
That's the end of my song.
  Ain't that odd?

There was a young girl in the choir,
Whose voice rose hoir and hoir,
Till she realized such a height
It was clear out of sight,
And they found it next day in the spoir.

A music critic who worked for the local newspaper, once wrote in a review: "The clarinet player did nothing all evening but stare at his navel."

In an early *Chicago Tribune* Sunday edition, the following announcement was seen: "Mrs. Elmo Spritz after Sunday services sang — "The Lord Knows Why.""

The Woes of a Music Teacher: Notes from Parents

My son cannot take piano lessons from you anymore. He's under the doctor's care. Please execute him.

To the High School band director: We resent your sending Charlie home because he has lice. If he does have them, he got them at your rehearsal room. And it's no wonder kids in there have lice with such a *lousy* band director as you leading them.

I'm sorry I missed the concert last Saturday but I was quite ill — the doctor shot me!

I wasn't at rehearsal last Wednesday because I had a bad case of intentional flu.

Please excuse my absence at last Sunday's concert. You see — I had loose vowels.

I resent your bawling me out before the entire orchestra for being late at rehearsal last Monday. I couldn't help it because I had an axadent that cut my foot.

Dear Conductor: I couldn't be with you yesterday because of going every ten minutes and I knew you wouldn't want me to have to go while in the orchestra.

Dear Tenye High School band director: You sent Eddie home because he smells. Well, he smells just like his father and I've had him for thirty years and he soots me just fine.

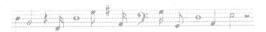

My son, Tommy, is under the Doctor's car and won't be attending practice for a few days.

Have you heard of the oboe player who wouldn't appear at orchestra practice very often during hunting season? He wrote this excuse: "Dear Director: Please excuse me from regular attendance at practice for the next few weeks because I'll be taking shots."

Dear Director: Please excuse me from orchestra practice on March 29, 30, 31, and 32.

Dear Choir Director: The wife and I have had bad colds and that's why I missed practice last Friday. Also, our telephone has been disconnected. Hope this finds you the same.

Dear Conductor: I was absent from rehearsal last Thursday with a sore throat, headache and chills. Our kids are also sick with fevers, and even my husband got hot last night.

Please excuse me for missing my lesson last week. I was homesick.

Doctor Roberts says Maria, our star soprano, is too fat. He wants to seduce her.

Please excuse my absence on June 16th at rehearsal. I had a bad cold and am still a little horse.

Please excuse me from rehearsal tomorrow (Jan 23) as I must go to the hospital to bring home my new son. I promise you that it won't happen again this season.

Please excuse my absence from rehearsal yesterday: I was absent because I didn't go.

Please excuse Tommy for missing band practice last Monday. But he had loose bowels and the doctor wanted a sample to examine for disease. I had to keep him home until he done it and that wasn't till five o'clock. That's why he missed school.

Please excuse Betty from glee club practice for the next few days. She is administrating; that's the reason.

More Musical Typos

Edgar Thomas, the violinist, was struck dead by a car at Fourth and Adams streets, just as the dead man attempted to cross.

The farewell party for Springfield's symphony conductor was a huge success.

Having broken both legs in a collision, our symphony's first violin chair is recovering under the car of her physician.

Teddy Conrad, the first clarinetist of the Danville Symphony Orchestra, is recovering from shock caused by touching a live wife.

You can count on it! Only a snake in the grass would attempt to knife a man in the back with so evil smelling a review.

Our glee club conductor, Charlie Hamm, was relieved of criminal jury duty yesterday because Hamm could not identify Yeggs.

Concert pianist Elmer Pletcher had a tragedy overtake him last Thursday. A dog chewed his windy finger. Pletcher, thinking the dog was poisoned, treated him but the dog did not respond to the anecdote.

CHAPTER 4

Opera, Voice, Songs, and Singers

Texas columnist George Fuermann tells of a Houston music lover who inquired in a music store for a record of a certain Bach chorale. The clerk said they didn't have any song about a back corral, but how would Deep In the Heart of Texas do?"

When in doubt, sing loud.

Robert Merrill

The softer you sing, the louder you're heard.

Donovan

Mrs. Jones, Mrs. Smith and Mrs. Brown were invited to the new home of Mrs. O'Brien for tea. When they were all seated awhile, Mrs. Smith excused herself to go to the ultra-modern bathroom, only to return soon, saying, "My dears, when I sat on the seat it played Beethoven! Can you imagine!"

Soon, Mrs. Brown excused herself and went to the ultra bathroom. She returned to say: "When I sat down it played a Chopin sonata."

Next, Mrs. Jones had to relieve herself, excused herself and went to the bathroom. She was so delayed in her return that Mrs. O'Brien went to see if all was well with her. She found Mrs. Jones wiping the floor and asked: "What went wrong here?"

"Wouldn't you know it — when I sat down, it played 'The Star Spangled Banner'."

Her singing was classic — mutiny on the high C's.

Every year the senior class at Riverton High School performed an opera. And one year, the script called for the soprano, the heaviest girl in the school, to collapse into the arms of the tiny tenor who was to lug her off stage.

Well, it didn't work out so well. The big girl dropped into the boy's arms perfectly but the kid almost collapsed. Still, he staggered toward the wings, painfully, inch-by-inch.

Then a voice from the audience was heard: "Hey, stupid, why don't you make two trips?"

Of all noises, I think music is the least disagreeable.

Samuel Johnson

Shortly after their annual concert the lead tenor in the school chorus approached the leader: "Golly, but that soprano who sang for you was just awful. Who was she?"

"She was my wife," was the leader's reply.

The kid blushed, gulped and managed to stammer: "Really — she wasn't all that bad, y'know. It was that miserable song she had to sing. Who could write such a bad song?"

"I did," replied the choral leader.

A baritone soloist sang 'I Will Not Pass This Way Again.' The audience was delighted.

Leo Slezak was performing *Lohengrin* and was almost done. He sang the words, "Mein Lieber Schwan," but the swan didn't appear! Slezak didn't falter, but turned to the audience and asked, "When does the next swan leave?"

A college student explained how he picked up a few dollars each week as an extra in the opera. "All I do," he laughed, "is carry a spear — and keep my mouth shut." "But after a hard day of classes, all that extra work!" gushed an elderly lady. "How do you keep awake?" "That's the least of my worries, lady," said the student. "The fellow behind me carries a spear, too!"

"George, I understand that you've been singing in the church choir. Is that correct?"

"Yep!"

"What part do you sing?"

"I sang tenor when I started but they changed that after they heard my voice."

"Really? What did you sing after that?"

"Short stop."

Nowadays, whatever ain't worth saying is sung.

A music critic, after seeing a performance of the opera *L'Enfant Prodigue*, said: "The only signs of a Biblical source were the fatted calves."

"Yeah, Yeah, Yeah!"

Reprinted with permission of
The Saturday Evening Post Society

One of the legendary opera stars, Mary Garden had an elderly "Sugar Daddy." One night he noticed that her dress was held up by only one strap. He asked: "What on earth holds your dress up, Mary?"

She replied, "Only one thing, Sir — your age."

In his autobiography *What Time's the Next Swan?*, Walter Slezak tells how his father, the famous opera star

Leo Slezak, was put on a strict diet because his weight had become excessive. For a week he moaned that he was being starved, then suddenly he began accepting his meager fare with readiness. But his dog betrayed him by taking a stand at Slezak's desk, and barking furiously. Mrs. Slezak investigated and found inside the desk a two-foot-long Italian sausage.

For showing up his master, Leo Slezak renamed his dog "Judas Iscariot."

Where did you learn to sing?
From correspondence school.
My, oh my. You must have missed a lot of mail.

Listening — Three shopgirls were enjoying a selection by the orchestra.

"Isn't it divine! Wonder what they're playing?" said Madge.

"It's the sextette from 'Lucia,'" announced Tillie positively.

"No, it's 'Tales of Hoffmann,'" persisted Annabelle.

"I think you are both wrong; but there's a card up there — I'll go and see for myself!" announced Madge, suiting the action to the word. She came back triumphant.

"You're way off, girls! It's the 'Refrain from Spitting.'"

"Honey, did you notice how my voice completely filled the auditorium last week at my concert?"

"I sure did, sweetheart. I also noticed several people leaving to make room for it."

"Yes, I'm an opera singer. But I can't live on income from that. On the side I'm a contortionist."

"Really? What's a contortionist?"

"I'm a guy who has to twist around here and there to make ends meet."

One of the basses in a men's glee club always sang fortissimo, to the distress of the rest of the club. Finally, one of them remarked to the fellow: "Last night I had an interesting dream. I dreamt that I heard a mighty choir with 10,000 sopranos, 8,000 altos and 7,000 tenors all singing at the top of their voices. And there you were with them, singing bass. And you know what? The conductor kept nodding to you and begging you: 'Don't sing so loud in the bass, please!'"

That did it. That guy never sang too loudly again.

Swans sing before they die, 'twere no bad thing should certain persons die before they sing.

Samuel Coleridge

It was the first time that Mrs. Arbutus's music class had ever been to an opera. The lights dimmed and the orchestra began to play with the conductor waving his baton furiously. The soprano began her solo.

Soon one student whispered a question to the teacher: "Why is that man throwing his stick toward that woman?"

"Oh, he's not trying to hit her, Elmer," chuckled the teacher.

"Then why is she screaming?"

At the opera the wife turned to her husband and said: "Don't you agree with me that the contralto has a heavenly voice?"

The husband replied: "I'm not sure of that — but it is unearthly."

This advertisement appeared in the "PERSONALS" column of the Greenwich Village, N.Y *Village Voice:* "After many years of constant study for the concert stage, I am now prepared to offer my services as an accomplished male baby-sitter."

"He likes classical music, art museums, and he reads a lot, but nobody's perfect."

Reprinted with permission of
The Saturday Evening Post Society

A famous opera star rests up between acts at the Met by performing Yoga exercises. "There's one person who gets a bigger kick out of this than I," he told a fellow artist, "and that's my little boy. I heard him explaining to a friend this morning, 'It's great when Daddy stands on his head. I grab money that falls out of his pockets and my dog licks his face.'"

One can't judge Wagner's opera, *Lohengrin*, after a first hearing! And I certainly don't intend hearing it a second time.

Gioacchino Rossini

The happening was inevitable: St. Peter High School was across the street from Memorial Medical Center where a woman was just emerging from anesthesia. As they wheeled her toward her room, she heard the band playing, "Heaven's Just Around the Corner."

"Now you take it easy, Ma'am," reassured the nurse, "That's just St. Peter's band."

The woman gasped: "You mean that I'm, that I'm —"

"No, I *don't* mean that!" the nurse reassured her.

After the concert, Mary Jones remarked to her friend: "Wasn't the repertoire of that soprano wonderfully extensive?"

Her friend replied: "It sure was. And that dress she had on made it even more so."

A pretty young singer went to see her doctor about her aches and pains. He carefully examined her and, finally, asked: "Do you know you've got acute appendicitis?"

"Oh, no! How terrible it is that I come here for an examination," the girl moaned, "and you get fresh with me!"

Baritone: "Last night at the concert I did myself proud. I held a note for over thirty-five seconds!"
Tenor: "Is that supposed to be sensational? Heck, my banker has held my note for three years!"

Sir Thomas Beecham was conducting a rehearsal of Massenet's *Don Quixote* in which Chaliapin, the Russian basso, was starring. At one point in the last act, the singer playing Dulcinea persistently failed to come in on the beat. "It's Mr. Chaliapin's fault," she protested at last. "He always dies too soon."

Walter Damrosch, composer of the opera *Cyrano De Bergerac*, arrived one day at the Met to see his opera. Because of the sudden illness of the tenor, *La Bohème* took the place of *Cyrano* but Damrosch was not informed of the switch. He sat quietly through the first act, then turned to the manager and demanded, "Who changed the scenery?"

Mrs. Glogauer, fat, rich, and fortyish, was about to give her first recital after years of arduous vocal lessons. The audience was large, if unenthusiastic, consisting of Mr. Glogauer's employees, who had been ordered to attend — or else.

"Oh," wailed the jittery Mrs. Glogauer, "if I only could learn what to do with my hands while I'm singing."

"Why not," suggested Mr. Glogauer wearily, "just hold them over your mouth?"

"So you went to the opera last night. Tell me — what did you hear?"

"Lotsa good stuff — the Smith's are getting a divorce, Susie Brown's pregnant and Elmer Bock just lost his job!"

It seems they have a good law in England that says a drunk can be arrested for singing. Whiskey affects different persons in different ways. Some get into a loving mood, some into a fighting mood, and some want to sing. The singing mood is the worst, and we'd rather fight a drunk than listen to him sing. It's something awful. We honestly believe that a recording of a drunk singing, played back to him next day, would do more to put him on the water-wagon than anything else.

Times
Thomasville, Ala.

There is a story about a certain opera impresario who was told that a prima donna he needed to sing for his opera wanted $5,000 a night. The guy grinned and said: "But I only want her to sing!"

Morris Fishbein tells of a man who bought his wife a piano for Christmas, but by Valentine's Day had persuaded her to switch to a clarinet. "How come?" asked a friend. "Well," was the explanation, "when she's playing the clarinet, she can't sing."

Texas columnist George Fuermann tells of a Houston music lover who inquired in a music store for a record of a certain Bach chorale. The clerk replied, "Gosh, we don't have any song about a back corral, but how would *Deep In the Heart of Texas* do?"

Victor Borge once told of a horse on stage during the opera *Aida* who dropped its load on stage! A professional critic murmured: "My God — what a critic!"

Q: Why did the music class hate their teacher?
A: She was just too...hot...tempoed.

Because an elderly Scotch lady had absorbed the ancient judgment that music in church was sinful, when she came to this country she refused to accept the general sentiment in favor of choir-singing.

In church the choir was singing an elaborate anthem which was new to her. Scowling, she turned to her neighbor and complained of the evil of modern ways which permitted a new-fangled piece of concert music in the sacred walls of a church. "But," protested her neighbor, "that anthem is very old and very sacred. Why, David sang it before Saul!" "Weel, weel," answered the old lady, "I understand now why Saul threw a javelin at David when the lad sang for him!"

My sister, when serving with the Red Cross in the South Pacific theater during World War II, was asked to sing at a GI entertainment one evening. The emcee introducing her told the audience that since formal evening dresses were hard to come by in the area, she had fashioned her gown from a parachute.

From the rear of the audience a voice boomed, "Where's the rip cord?"

This is a fault common to all singers that among their friends they never are inclined to sing when they are asked: unasked, they never desist.

"E above high C."

In a church in Ohio, the minister gave out the hymn "Love to Steal Away." The regular leader of the choir being absent, the duty devolved upon a shy young fellow who began the hymn. He began, "I love to steal," and then broke down. Raising his voice a bit higher, he sang, "I love to steal." At length, after a desperate cough, he roared out, "I love to steal." The effort was too much. Everyone but the parson was laughing. The parson with utmost gravity, said: "Seeing our brother's preferences, let us pray."

"George — we really miss you. Why did you quit singing in the church choir?"

"Because one day I didn't show up for practice and somebody asked if the organ had been fixed."

A New York show girl covered in a new mink coat encountered some old friends who complimented her on the new fur coat. "Oh, this," she said coyly, shrugging her shoulders. "I got it for a mere song."

"Song?" repeated one friend. "Looks more like an overture to me!"

After *Pelleas Melisande* was performed at the Boston Opera, several customers demanded a refund of their money because they had expected a double feature, the one *Pelleas*, and the other *Melisande*!

"Somehow your voice puts me in mind of sailors aboard ship."

"How strange! Can you explain that?"

"Sure. Your voice has a tendency to die on the high C."

Guest at a musicale: "That's very difficult, hard music that contralto is struggling with!"
Other guest: *"Difficult?* Too bad it ain't *impossible!"*

Pretty young student: "Professor Aaron, do you think my voice will ever amount to anything?"
Weary teacher: "Well it might come in handy in case of fire or shipwreck."

At the private party, the host turned to the town's leading tenor saying, "Now folks, let's have a song from our friend Elmore Adams."
"I'm sure sorry, folks, but the only time I sing is when I'm in the bathtub."
"We understand that, Elmore — I'll just tell the folks that you're out of practice."

In the telephone booth, the patron addressed the telephone: "I'd like tickets for the opera tonight. I'd like a box for two."
"I'm sorry, but we don't have boxes for two."
"What? Ridiculous. Aren't you the box office?"
"No — we're the undertaker."

"You've got to smell a lot of mule manure before you can sing like a hillbilly"

Hank Williams
(1923-1953)

The Mixed Chorus

This motley mass we see before us —
This odd array — is called a CHORUS,
Or Glee Club, Choral Group or Choir,
Which Bach and Beethoven desire.
Sopranos, Altos, Tenors, Basses
Are rarely chosen for their faces
But for the strength which they employ
In shrieking out "The Hymn of Joy."
The keen-eyed listener often sees
Impending tonsillectomies.
Or hears the twanging of the hordes
Of taut (and untaught) vocal cords.
One thing seems definitely certain
They should perform behind a curtain
And change the adage then to mean:
"Choruses should be heard not seen."

Laurence McKinney, *People of Note*
(Out of print for nearly 30 years, will be re-released in
1999. If you can't locate a copy, try Amazon.com on the
internet)

Voice floating out of the opera singer's dressing room: "I'm *not* conceited, although gosh knows I have every reason to be!"

The pretty young lady was drumming on the piano while she hummed a tune. Her beau sat beside her and soon inquired: "Do you sing and play a lot?"

"No, I just do it to kill time," she replied.

"Well, I must say you've got a first class weapon for it," remarked her beau. (We'd guess he wasn't her beau for long, wouldn't you agree?)

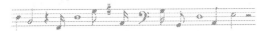

"Can you name the most fearsome, affecting, even devastating, war music ever written?"

"Sure can. 'Here Comes The Bride' is the title."

The great diva Madame Schumann Heicke was simply enormous, a huge gargantuan woman. One time, trying to squeeze through the narrow aisle to get to the front of the stage, bumping the violins and cellos en route, she was told by a violinist: "Madame, try going through the aisle sideways."

"But I am going through sideways," said Madame Schumann Heicke.

The young lady was being auditioned and as she sang, the auditor wriggled uncomfortably in his seat. During a lull in the song, he asked the singer: "How much of the song have you sung?" She replied, "I've sung down to where it says 'refrain'."

"Then I'd suggest that you follow that direction, Ma'am."

The church choir had just gotten a new singer, who, during the song allowed her voice to soar above all the others, dimming every voice but hers.

After the concert, one soprano asked the tenor what he thought of the new addition to the choir. He said: "That girl has the most selfish voice I have ever heard!"

A Russian pianist was engaged by a wealthy would-be soprano to accompany her at a concert. During rehearsals the pianist suddenly threw up his hands in despair, saying: "I geev op, Madam. Eeeet ees no use. I blay the black keyes, I blay the vite keys — und all you do ees seeng een da cracks!"

"Henry! Are you listening or are you just thinking?"

Castrado: A man who has had his works cut out for him.
                                                  Robert Byrne

"My daughter is going to Europe to complete her musical voice education."

"Really! But that's so expensive. Where did you get the money to send her?"

"I didn't get it. The neighbors chipped in."

A man was attending the opera with his friend but after the start of the final act he was overcome with a burning thirst. He stood and went to an usher and asked for the location of the drinking fountain. The usher gave such elaborate, difficult and misunderstood directions that the guy had an impossible time trying to follow the usher's instructions. But, at last, lo and behold, he came to a flowing stream flowing out of a large fountain, where he knelt and began to drink the flowing water. Finished, he went back to his seat next to his friend. "Did I miss much?" he asked.

"Hardly anything. You were part of the scene most of the time."

Q: What's the difference between an alto and a baritone?

A: Almost sixty pounds.

"Did you hear about the singer who imitated Bing Crosby?"

"Nope, sure didn't. What happened?"

"He drowned. He was on a boat and it sank! His problem was that he kept swimming in circles to stay in the spotlight."

The couple was at the opera but couldn't really enjoy it because the couple behind them kept talking during the performance. Turning around, the man said, "Excuse me, Sir, but we can't hear a word!"

The man replied: "It's honestly not your business *what* I'm telling my wife!"

Agent to customer who needs a singer for a forthcoming private party:

"Allow me to suggest Madame Dupreyst."

"Is her voice quite good?"

"Good! Why you must have heard that she's a recognized Diva."

"Never mind about her morals. Can she sing?"

It was an amateur voice concert and one young lady came on stage and announced that the audience would have to excuse her voice because she had a slight cold. Then she began to sing: "I'll hang my harp on an Elm tree-e-e, brppp, Oh!" Four times more she tried to make the high note, but each time her voice broke. A voice from the audience called out: "Young lady, try hanging it on a lower branch!"

What is the most popular song among little monsters? "Thank Heaven for Little Ghouls!"

When Lucy Monroe gives with the high notes of the "Star Spangled Banner," the lyrics come across as clear as a bell. Obviously, there was nobody like her around when former columnist Franklin P. Adams was a lad. He confessed that until he reached the age of twelve, he was convinced that the first line of our anthem was, "Osage, Kansas City."

George Bernard Shaw gave his opinion about Gounod's *La Redemption*: "If one will only take the precaution to go in long enough after it commences and to come out long before it is over, you will not find it wearisome."

One man admits that he always goes to the front porch when his wife, an aspiring soprano, practices. "That's because," the husband explains, "I don't want the neighbors to think I'm beating her!"

The true, real, unhypocritical wife is the one who loves voice music sufficiently to applaud her husband when be comes home at 7 A.M., drunk and singing a tenor song.

In America our popular songs have an almost tragic shortness of life. A cynic remarked on that fact: "That's because so many singers, orchestras and instrumentalists murder them!"

The industry's report has it that country music records sell better than recordings of any other type of music. One wonders if the reason for that isn't because when the singers are worn out, you don't know it.

The *San Francisco Medical Journal* reported that:
"Singing is, in certain cases of deafness, extremely
beneficial."

The editor added, below the statement: "And we might
add a 'vice versa' to that!"

Neighbor: "We'd love to have you come over to our
house and sing for our party Saturday night."

Singer: "How nice! Do you truly like my voice that
much?"

Neighbor: "Nope! But we're looking for ways to break our
lease."

"Isn't she feeling well, or is it that Frank Sinatra?"

Reprinted with permission of
The Saturday Evening Post Society

A critic wrote of a Broadway musical: "I must admit that I saw the show under unfortunate circumstances — the curtain was up!"

Mary: "Why was Daddy singing to our baby tonight?"
Mommy: "Because he wanted to sing her to sleep, that's why."
Mary: "Gosh, if I was a baby, I'd sure pretend I WAS asleep."

Q: Why was the bass singer kicked out of his choir class?
A: Because he was always sliding into treble.

A critic is like a legless man who teaches running.
                                        Channing Pollack
                                                  (1888)

I am sitting in the smallest room of my house. I have your review before me. In a moment it'll be behind me.
                                              Max Keger
                                            (1873-1906)

How do you irritate a soprano?
Ask her to read the music!

A famous tenor was singing *Faust* on the stage of the Boston Opera House, but the stage was inadequately equipped for the performance. The trap door was supposed to sink down so that Mephistopheles could conduct Faust into Hell. But as the tenor stepped on the trap door and began to sink, the door malfunctioned and left the singer stranded half up and half down. The audience stirred, murmured, then suddenly a voice rose above the disturbance yelling: "I'm safe at last — HELL — IS — FULL!"

"That contralto certainly has a singular voice!"
"That's for sure. But aren't you glad it's not plural?"

There are some experiences in life which should not be demanded twice from any man, and one of them is listening to the *Brahms Requiem*.

George Bernard Shaw
(1856-1950)

That gal has everything a singer should have. And her voice ain't bad either! Why, she sings southern songs so naturally that when they hear her — folks put cotton in their ears.

What is the favorite song of a female ghost?
Demons are a ghoul's best friend!

There is a special way to put a glint and a twinkle in an alto's eye. First get a flashlight — then shine it in her ear.

There is nothing in the world I wouldn't do for Bob Hope, and there is nothing he wouldn't do for me. We spend our days doing nothing for each other.

Bing Crosby
(1904-77)

The story is told of how the great Charlie Chaplin was once at a party and imitating famous people. Suddenly he began to sing with a voice sonorous and lovely. "Why, Charlie," yelled one of his friends, "I didn't know you could sing."

"I can't," Charlie replied, "I'm just imitating Caruso."

We rarely hear the loveliest sound of all — the sound of the songs at falling prices.

Some of these soap operas are incredible. One show concerns a murderer, a drug addict, an unfaithful wife, a bank robber, an adulterer and an unwed mother. And the title? "Just Plain Folks."

It is simply ridiculous to say that soap operas are true to life. When did you ever have a thirty-minute argument with your wife!

"Pete sang a solo with accompaniment from his glee club last night."

"That's miraculous! Why, that Pete can't sing worth a dern. Who egged him on to do it?"

"We don't know. But he's looking for the guy who egged him off!"

"Let's all stand now, and murder Hymn 147..."

An ancient musician named Gluck
The manner Italian forsook.
    He fought with Puccini,
        Gave way to Rossini,
            You can find all his views in a buck.

A guy goes into a bird store and says, "I want a singing canary."

"We've got a great one. He sings like Caruso, sings like no other bird in the world — uses marvelous improvisations. He's worth a thousand dollars."

"That's a lot of money, but if he sings like Caruso, I'll buy him."

"Good, but you've got to take the other bird with him."

The buyer looks at the other bird who had lost half his feathers, with pus around his eyes and looked sick. "But why do I have to take him?" he asked.

"Because he's the arranger!" was the reply.

Old Songs: They are the best of all songs because nobody sings them anymore.

Coming home from the opera, Hubby said "Maybelle, I sure admire that guy who sang the tenor part."

Maybelle: "Really? I certainly didn't. I thought he had an awful voice."

Hubby: "Yes and so did I. But just consider the nerve, the audacity, the sheer courage of that guy to sing with a voice like that."

"Did you go to hear that soprano sing in concert, last night? Didn't she have a most singular voice?"

"I'll say. And I'll also say: 'Thank God it wasn't plural!'"

A singer asked his voice teacher: "Do you think I'll ever be able to use my voice in concert?"

"I don't know about concerts," his teacher responded, "But it'll come in handy in case of a fire."

97

A tenor from Idaho's Boise,
Has a voice no one out there enjoysees,
He can practice all day,
And be heard miles away,
And he's still much too noisy for Boise.

"If I had the power I would insist that all oratorios be sung in the costume of the period, with the possible exception of *The Creation.*"

Earnest Newman

"What I love best about opera is the women who listen to it."

Jules Goucourt

A well-known coloratura soprano went to her physician for a medical examination.

"Please remove your blouse," the doctor ordered.

"Oh no! Anything but that," exclaimed the singer, concerned with showing her flat chest.

"Come, come now," advised the physician. "Let's not make mountains out of molehills!"

Her soprano voice was remarkably bad — the kind of voice the undertaker uses to augment grief at a funeral.

One time an Arkansas farmer who was deacon in his church was called to serve on a federal grand jury in nearby

Little Rock. He was gone three weeks and when he got home, the first thing his wife asked him was: "Honey, did you know any of the songs they sang in that Little Rock Church on Sunday mornings?"

"Nope," husband replied: "They didn't sing no songs, just anthems."

"Anthems? Good gravy, what's anthems?"

"I'll try to explain it to ya," hubby said. "Now, Maw, if'n I was to say — 'Maw, them cows is in the corn', that wouldn't be no anthem."

"Don't suppose so," responded Maw.

"But if'n I was to say in a long, shakery voice, 'Maw, Maw, Maw, them cows, them horny cows like that Jersey or that Holstein, or Old Billy — all them cows is in — is in — them cow-ow-ows is in the — in the — in the corn, the corn, thet fields cor-r-rn, ahmen, ahmen, ah-h-h-hmen,' now *that* would be an anthem."

Lots of girls can be had for a song, but the only problem with that is the song is a wedding march.

"Often a song that fails completely is given a brand-new title by its composer and publisher and then promptly scores a smash hit," notes Louis Sobol. "Make Me a Star," for instance, renamed "Blue Moon," quickly made the Hit Parade. Other temporary flops that followed a similar pattern were: "Turkish Tom Tom" changed to "Dardanella," "Smile and Show Your Dimple" renamed "Easter Parade," "If I Were on the Stage" changed to "Kiss Me Again," and "I Have No Words," republished as "Something to Remember You By."

Lonie and Sarah were celebrating their 30th wedding anniversary by going to the movies. Sarah's eyes filled with tears as Nelson Eddy sang "Indian Love Call" to Jeanette MacDonald:

"When I'm calling you-oo-oo-ou-hoo-hoo-hooo —"

Sarah took Lonie's hand, saying, "Oh, you sweet! When a man has love in his heart, that song shows what happens to him."

"No, it don't!" snapped Lonie. "He just ran out of words before he ran out of music!"

The stage is bad, so purists say,
  and only evil from it springs.
But it has what angels have
  and purists lack it, too.
Namely, wings!

"Mr. Evans, isn't that tenor's voice glorious? That man can hold a note for almost a minute."

"I know him quite well. I'm his banker and I've held his note for two years."

Mrs. Amos was in her fifties, quite hefty and even more wealthy. She began to take voice lessons and was about to have her first concert. Backstage she confided to a friend that her hands — her hands — she just didn't know what to do with them when she began to sing.

"I'll tell you what to do," her friend whispered. "Just hold them over your mouth!"

"I have an act I think you could use," the man said to the TV producer.

From one pocket he took a mouse and a miniature piano, which he placed on the producer's desk. Out of the other he took a beautiful butterfly. At once the mouse began to play and the butterfly began to sing.

"That is absolutely sensational," the producer said. "Name your price."

"Well," said the man, "there is one thing you should know. The act really isn't as good as it seems. You see, the butterfly really can't sing. The mouse is doing it. You see he is a ventriloquist."

The famous singer Enrico Caruso was driving through the Ozark country on his way to St. Louis for a concert. Suddenly, he realized that he was lost! So, he stopped at a farmhouse to ask directions and during the conversation said he'd like a drink of water. The farmer fetched him a drink and invited him to stay for dinner. During the meal, he told the couple who he was and the farmer was overjoyed.

"How wonderful!" the farmer exclaimed. "Just think of me, a hick from Hicksville, having a guest as famous as Robinson Carusoe."

Palestrina? Of course I know about her. She was born in Jerusalem.

"You say you went to the concert hall yesterday? And what did you hear?"

"I heard some fascinating stuff: Elmer Jenkins is going broke, Pete Simpson now wears a wig, and the Rogers are getting a divorce."

"My daughter is taking voice lessons."

"And how is she getting along?"

"Her voice steadily gets stronger. She used to be heard only in the apartment next door. But now, after two years of voice lessons, we get complaints from neighbors three and four buildings away!"

A well-known coloratura soprano is reputed to have a willowy figure, cherry-red lips, chestnut hair and hazel eyes. She grew up on a tree farm.

Little Eddie enjoyed singing no less than his grandfather enjoyed accompanying him on the piano.

One evening the folks had company and they asked the boy to sing for them. He did just that while grandpa accompanied him and played as softly as possible so as not to interfere with the boy's little voice.

Suddenly the kid quit singing, turned to his Grandfather and said, "Hey, Grandpop, give her more gas!"

"Where did you learn to sing?"

"From correspondence school."

"My, oh my. You must have missed a lot of mail."

The soprano had just finished a long, high-toned number and one of the audience asked his seatmate, "I sure think she's a totally finished singer, don't you?"

"I sure hope so, but it looks like she's going to sing again!"

Along about 1930, a young man named Irving Caesar wrote the lyrics for a song he hoped would make him famous. It was called "Louisville," and wasn't very good. The point of this story, however, is that Caesar persuaded a composer named J. Fred Cootes to set the words of "Louisville" to music — and Cootes' melody was very good indeed.

In fact, Cootes remembered the melody some four years later when another lyricist named Gillespie popped up with lyrics that impressed everybody in Caesar's office. The words of the new song and the melody written for "Louisville" fitted together like ham and eggs, or Scotch and soda — and the result was published just in time for the holiday season of 1934. It has sold over a million records and copies of sheet music every year since, and promises to go on for many years more. The song: "Santa Claus Is Coming to Town."

When Arthur Godfrey was a record jockey, he told a devoted listener that he had dedicated a new song to her. The title: "I'll Send You a Kitten, Dear. You Need a New Puss!"

Modern Music: It's played so fast and hot that you can't tell what song is being played nor can you tell what song it was stolen from.

Johnny Jumpdown had his first voice concert in Key West and THAT was the first time ever that he knew what "key" he was in.

Having the critics praise you is like having the hangman say you have a pretty neck.

Eli Wallach

Little Johnny was with his mother at the opera, Johnny's first opera ever. As the celebrated soprano began her aria, Johnny turned to his mother and asked: "Why is that man who's standing in front of her with his back to us, shaking his stick at her?"

"Quiet, Johnny," his mother whispered back. "He's not shaking his stick at her."

"He's got to be shaking it at her, or else why would she be hollering so loud?"

During rehearsals for the Verdi opera *Otello*, the director demanded that the tenor interrupt his climactic moment in a song to get to the back of the stage during only a short rest in the action and while the chorus was singing. The tenor saw no point in this action and told the director that, but the director insisted time after time that he should go to the back of the stage and return at the climactic moment. The director insisted: "You must do it because that's the tradition for the opera. Tamango created the role and he always went to the back of the stage at this time in the music." The tenor's protest did no good.

Some time later, the singer was in Italy and went to see the famous Tamango and asked him about this break to go to the back of the stage in the climactic part of the opera.

Tamango couldn't remember but he looked at the pages of the score and then said, "Now I remember. It's simple. You recall that in the final passage Otello must sing a high B flat. So, while the chorus was singing, I went to spit."

He's a lousy singer but folks like to see his Adam's Apple bob up and down!

Ambitious, inexperienced vocalist: "As my teacher, do you think I'll ever be able to do anything with my voice?"
　　"It should alert people if you happen to use it at a fire or bank robbery!"

A famous baritone was in his agent's office, having a discussion about salary. He kept his hand cupped behind his ear trying to hear better. "I'm getting a tad hard of hearing," he said, "all that applause, don'tcha know."

A man said to his buddy, "I read in the paper this morning that singing warms the blood. His buddy replied, "I believe it because I've heard singin that made my blood boil!"

It's unfortunate that the life of a popular song is brief, but, on the other hand, it's just as well forgotten so that the next generation can't use it against us.

There once was a young fellow named Jenner,
Who sang a phenomenal tenor,
He had little to spend
So I often would lend
The tenor a ten or a tenner.

Carolyn Wells
Book of American Limericks (1925)

Have you heard of the Near-Sighted Association? They have a special theme song! Title? "I've Lost My Glasses and Wonder Who's Kissing Her Now."

He was a composer who aspired to write drinking songs but he failed because he couldn't get past the first few bars.

I love a finished baritone,
I honestly, honestly do.
I don't mean a guy who's polished,
I point to the one who's through.

                                        Author unknown

When the monster graduated from college he sang this song to his parents: "Hey folks, I want a ghoul just like the ghoul that married dear old Dad."

A famous coloratura soprano was having an argument with her agent over inadequate fees. "Madam," replied the agent, "you are now making more money than the President of the United States."

"If that's so," replied the singer, "why don't you just go and get him to sing for you."

Growing old has at least one advantage — you can sing while you brush your teeth.

There was an old lady named Marta
Who was quite an accomplished farter
She could fart anything from "You're My Everything"
To Beethoven's "Moonlight Sonata."

Voice: When a woman lowers her voice it signals she wants something. When she raises it, that signals she didn't get it.

Q: "What did Juliet say to Romeo when she met him in the balcony?"
A: "Couldn't you have gotten seats in the orchestra!"

A confirmed bachelor has been defined as one who sings songs like WINE, WOMEN AND SO LONG.

Q: "How do you get a coloratura soprano into a compact car?"
A: "Grease her hips and put a piece of pie on the dashboard!"

Wife: "The paper says that the concert we went to last night was a great success."
Husband: "Really? I had no idea we enjoyed it that much."

A baritone soloist sang: "I Will Not Pass this Way Again." The audience was delighted.

M is the Man in the Moon,
Who sings a remarkable tune.
It begins in high C
and then runs back to D
I should think not a moment too soon.

A cure for drunkenness that needs to be far better known and used is the one that records a drunk singing and then plays it back to him the next day.

"That soprano has a huge repertoire, doesn't she?"
"She sure does — and that dress of hers makes it look even more huge!"

Yep! He's pretty well-known. He's sung on TV, stage, and screen. There is just no way to escape him!

A folk singer is someone who sings through his nose by ear.

Barbra Streisand, she of the magnificent voice, was looking for a present for a friend. She walked into the Farmers' Market in Los Angeles where she took a fancy to a parrot for sale in a special cage. She asked, "Can he fly?"
"Oh yes," replied the salesman. "Unless he takes the train!"

Song Writer: One who is calm and composed.

It is said that the most difficult thing about writing a drink-ing song is the matter of getting past the first bar.

After his medical check-up for a cardiac problem, he asked to have the long strip of celluloid that had all kinds of odd markings on it. The doctor allowed him to take the strip home.

Once home, the patient left the strip on the table and went to the store. When he returned, the celluloid strip — the cardiogram — was gone. He called to his wife: "Honey, did you move my cardiogram strip?"

"Yes," she replied, "I put it on our antique player piano and it played the song wonderfully well."

"What? What song?"

"Nearer My God to Thee!"

I saw that opera under simply intolerable conditions — the curtain was up!

Some guys are just unbelievably arrogant and conceited. Consider the case of the policeman who died and went to heaven. He had become a bass singer. Now he stood before the Pearly Gates and an angel asked him: "Is there a particular item or wish for you?"

"Yep!" replied the cop, "I like choir singers and their music. Get me five thousand choir singers."

"Well, I can do that for you," responded the angel. "Anything else?"

"Five thousand tenors, too," said the cop. "And that'll do for now."

"But how about the basses?" asked the angel.

"Never mind that," he replied, "I'll sing bass."

Opportuneshark: A writer of derivative music.

He's a very inventive guy. He even invented a double-decker bathtub for people who want to sing duets while bathing.

They say that the only music Americans will stand for at any and all times is the "Star-Spangled Banner."

Americans stand when they hear the words of the "Star Spangled Banner," but they fall when they try to sing it.

All of a sudden the great Prima Donna cried,
"Heavens, my voice is a goner!"
But a cat in the wings said,
"I know how she sings,"
And finished the solo with honor.

Carolyn Wells
Book of American Limericks (1925)

"A soap opera is corn on the sob."

Tosca

Most such operatic disasters depend on some element of misunderstanding and incompetence among the stage-management, this catastrophe is due entirely to ill-will, in this case between the stage staff and the soprano. With diabolical cunning they permitted her, after several stormy rehearsals, to complete her first performance without mishap until the very last moment, when Tosca throws herself off the battlements of the Castel Sant'Angelo. What normally happens is that on her cry *'Scarpia davanti a Dio'* she hurls herself off and lands on a mattress three feet below. In this case the large young American who landed not on a mattress, but-perish the thought-on a *trampoline*. It is said that she came up fifteen times before the curtain fell — sometimes upside down, then the right way up — now laughing in delirious glee, now screaming with rage — Worse still, it seems that the unhappy lady was unable to reappear in any other Opera Center performance throughout the entire season because the Center's faithful audience, remembering the trampoline, would have burst into laughter. She had to remove herself to San Francisco, where of course no such grotesque incident could possibly occur —

Giacomo Puccini
City Center, New York 1960

People who have heard me sing say I don't.

Mark Twain

Barber shop quartet: "Four male singers who just never got waited on."

I do not care what language an opera is sung in so long as it is in a tongue I don't understand.

No decent opera plot can be sensible, for people do not sing when they feel sensible.

W.H. Auden
quoted in *Time* 1961

Don Giovanni

Many operas end like *Tosca* with the sudden descent of the hero to some nether realm. Don Giovanni, however (as in Zeffirelli's production for Covent Garden), tends simply to disappear amid whirling clouds of stage-smoke as the chorus of off-stage demons promise him worse torments below. In Vienna, however, Cesare Siepi ended his admirable interpretation standing on a stagelift which, as so often happened, stuck halfway down, leaving his head and shoulders visible to the audience but not the rest of him. The technicians' efforts merely revealed the operation of one of the great laws governing opera disasters–that the most that can be hoped for is to restore the *status quo ante*–that is, they merely brought him back up again. Siepi then amazed the public by refusing simply to walk off and with courageous professionalism challenged the lift-operator to a second attempt. Of course, exactly the same thing happened, and amid the shocked silence of the Staatsoper a single voice rang out–it is said in Italian — 'Oh my God, how wonderful — Hell is full.'

W.A. Mozari
Vienna State Opera, 1958

Opera in English is, in the main, just about as sensible as baseball in Italian.

H.L. Mencken

A young lady who sings in our choir
Whose hair is the color of phoir
But her charm is unique,
She has such a flair chique,
It is really a joy to be nigh her.

Carolyn Wells
Book of American Limericks 1925

The Third Verse Of "America"

We were on our way to Raleigh. The expedition had been arranged for the exclusive purpose of letting the children see the exhibit in the State Museum. For a month or more they had been begging to take the trip, so a date was set and we left home bright and early in order that their desire might be satisfied.

All this happened while we were living down in Washington, D.C., before moving to Raleigh. The children were much younger then.

Mrs. Goerch and I were on the front seat: the children occupied the rear seat.

It was after we passed Farmville that they started singing by way of amusing themselves. Following the rendition of several new songs which they recently had learned in school, they branched off into "America." The first verse was negotiated successfully, and so was the second. It was when they tried to start the third that all the trouble began.

"How does it go, mother?" asked Doris.

"How does what go?" inquired mother, who hadn't been paying much attention to what was going on.

"How does the third verse of 'America' start?"

"Let's see: doesn't it go like this: 'I love thy rocks and rills?'"

"No!" she exclaimed indignantly. "We just sang that: it's part of the second verse."

" 'Long may our land be bright,'" I suggested.

"That isn't right either," said Sibyl.

"I believe it's something about 'Let rocks their silence break'," advised mother.

That sounded as though it might work, but when they started singing it, they found it couldn't be made to fit, so they were forced to toss the suggestion aside.

It's funny how a thing like that can stay with you. You get all stirred up and can't feel contented and at peace until you have reached a satisfactory solution of whatever proposition it is that happens to be puzzling you. We debated and discussed the song for fifteen or twenty minutes and still were entirely at a loss. Just about that time we were nearing a farm-house, close by the side of the highway. A man was asleep on the porch, a big straw hat shading his face. He lay on the floor of the porch, his knees drawn up and his bare toes protruding over the edge. Probably he had been plowing out in the field and had decided to rest a little before continuing his labors.

I applied the brakes and brought the car to a stop. My wife and children wanted to know what was going on, but I paid them no mind. I hollered to the man on the porch and at the second yell he raised himself to an erect posture.

"Howdy!" I greeted him.

He rubbed his eyes sleepily and returned my greeting.

"Can you tell me how the third verse of 'America' starts?" I inquired politely.

"Huh?"

"Do you know the words of the third verse of 'America'?"

"America?"

"Yes. How does the third verse go?"

"The third verse?"

His mental machinery evidently was operating in low gear.

"Can you sing the third verse of "My Country 'tis of Thee?" I inquired patiently.

There was a note of horror in his voice as he said: "Can I sing what?"

I saw we never would get any information there, so I threw the car in gear again and resumed our drive to Raleigh. When we had gone a short distance up the road, I looked back and saw the man still sitting there, gazing fixedly in our direction with amazement written all over his countenance.

I'd be willing to bet he didn't sleep any more that day.

Mrs. Goerch and the children, who had been too scared up to that time to make any comments, had quite a lot to say about it. They insisted I let the matter drop.

I did, for a while, but I couldn't keep the thing off my mind. There was a policeman at Capitol Square in Raleigh who looked rather intelligent so I stopped the car and beckoned him to come over. He did, and I asked him whether he knew the third verse of "America." He said rather gruffly that he couldn't sing a note. While he was saying it, he leaned over so he could sniff my breath.

One of the clerks at Boylan Peace's store also professed her ignorance, as likewise did an elderly gentleman who I found in front of the dry goods counter. By that time Mrs. Goerch and the children refused to stay in my company any longer and insisted that I leave them.

I did, and when I got out on Fayetteville Street, one of the first persons I met was Tom Bost, who for many years was correspondent for the *Greensboro Daily News*.

"Tom," I greeted him, "how does the third verse of 'America' go?"

Right away I saw a difference in the make-up of a newspaperman and the average run of people. Everybody else whom I had asked the question had stared at me in amazement. Tom didn't do any such thing. He seemed to think it was the most natural thing in the world, and he stood in the middle of the sidewalk, thinking profoundly.

"Let me see," he finally said. "I can't just exactly recall, but if I sing the first two verses, perhaps the third will come to me."

He started off with "My country 'tis of thee." He really had a good voice and I listened appreciatively as he went through the first two verses without a hitch. So did several other people who happened to be passing by. Some of them stopped. Tom came to the end of the second verse, remained silent for a moment or two and then admitted his defeat.

"Darned if I can think of it to save my life," he confessed. "But let's go in here a minute."

We went into a drugstore and he asked three of the

clerks and four or five customers, but none of them knew. We stopped in several other stores and wound up at the Sir Walter Hotel. Tom introduced me to a professor of music — Dingley Brown, I believe he said was the name — but he was just as ignorant as everyone else.

By this time Tom was just as keenly interested as I was, and when we finally parted, he announced he was going around to Alfred Williams' store and look up the song.

My folks were about ready to leave by then, so I had to wait until we got back home before I could satisfy my curiosity. They swore they wouldn't speak to me for a week if I asked anyone else along the way, so I didn't.

The minute we got home, I looked through a songbook and found what I wanted. I sang the third verse and quick as a flash the rest of the family caught on, and we sang the song through to the very end.

by Carl Goerch
Just for the Fun of It
Raleigh, N.C., 1954

The contralto found a baby on her doorstep and adopted it. The orchestra called the baby her "stepson."

The first act of the opera occupied three hours, and I enjoyed that in spite of the singing.

A Tramp Abroad
Mark Twain
(1835-1910)

Her voice sounded like a Canada Goose actually being goosed!

The opera is to music what a bawdy house is to a cathedral.

H.L. Mencken

People are wrong when they say that opera is not what it used to be. It is what it used to be. That is what is wrong with it.

Noel Coward

Saturday nights are usually reserved for dining and dancing, but not always. There are households in Dixie where country music reigns supreme on Saturday nights when the radio is tuned to WSM in Nashville, Tennessee, the Grand Ole Opry station. Turning the dial to 650-AM is automatic. Yep, Saturday nights are syrup and biscuits and country ham and red-eye gravy and grits and Grand Ole Opry.

The folks in Dixie grew up and swore by the likes of Red Foley, Cowboy Copas, Carl Smith, Webb Pierce, Roy Acuff, Hank Snow, Ernest Tubb, Rod Brasfield, "The Duke of Paducah," Minnie Pearl, "Little Jimmy" Dickens, Hank Williams, Eddy Arnold, Chet Atkins, "Stringbean," Homer and Jethro, The Carter Family, Johnny Cash, Patsy Cline, Tom T. Hall, Lester Flatt, The Jordanaires, Bill Monroe and The Bluegrass Boys, Uncle Dave Macon, Kitty Wells, The Bailes Brothers, Lonzo and Oscar and a host of others.

Hell, they were family!

Country music sends out a message. The performers sing words, not lyrics. They sing words that mean something and echo a message a fella' can understand and relate to. They'll make you cry, and laugh; remember and forget; cuss and pray.

My good friend Lewis Grizzard, premier columnist for the *Atlanta Constitution*, is a good ol' boy from Moreland, Georgia. He's a dyed-in-the-wool country music fan and will bring tears to your eyes when he relates how country music saved his life in the desolate, cold and unfriendly atmosphere of Chicago.

"I was homesick and lonely. My wife had backed a truck up to the apartment and cleaned me out. She took everything but the blame, including my dog. An' I'll tell you this, any woman who'll take y'r dog'll cutcha'. I realized that the only person who loved me was my mama, an' she was 800 miles away in Georgia. So I reached for the only thing I had left, my country music albums. I selected one at random, without looking at the title, and dropped it on the turntable of my stereo. The reassuring words rendered forth as I gazed out my window at a cold, snowy day in Chicago, 'You tore my heart out an' stomped that sucker flat'."

Two other Grizzard favorites are, "Don't Give Me No Plastic Saddle, Baby — I Want to Feel that Leather When I Ride," and "Mama's Cookin', Daddy's Jukin' — An' The Baby's Eatin' the Fly Swatter Again."

Still another lifelong lover of country music is Ludlow Porch from Snellville, Georgia. Ludlow is known and loved by all as "Mr. Radio" in Atlanta, where he holds forth daily doing a five-hour talk show on WSB-AM.

"Shoot, I was a country music fan long before it was fashionable," Porch allows. "Heck, I was listenin' to country music when Dolly Parton was still wearin' a trainin' bra; when Porter Waggoner was a trusty. What I'm sayin' is, I was a country music fan when Donnie and Marie wore braces on their teeth, an' when Oral Roberts was goin' to a chiropractor. I love country music because country music singers sing words that tug at your heart-strings; words that make you want to cry; words that make you want to go right out an' beat up a Commie. I'm talkin' 'bout beautiful, meaningful words like, 'Our Marriage Was a Failure, But Our Divorce Ain't Workin' Out Either', 'Hold My Beer, Leon, While I Knee Jane Fonda', and 'Bobby Joe, Your Wife Is Cheatin' on Us Again'."

'Nother thing, down here in Dixie we have country music rednecks, male and female, who tithe with regularity. Ten percent of everything they make goes in the jukebox. Their theory is that "If Willie Nelson says it, it's true."

What, really is country music? Just this:

Country music is more than entertainment, more than pickin' and grinnin', more than two-for-a-quarter selections on a juke box in some remote honky-tonk or truck stop. It is more than a concert in the local high school auditorium, more than Willie Nelson going one-on-one on the radio with an over-the-road trucker at midnight bound from Atlanta to Houston. It is more than a Saturday night dance at the VFW, more than music to work and play by.

In Dixie, country music is a way of life, and to some almost a religion. It is just as southern as grits, hot biscuits, and redeye gravy. It bares the facts of life, the good and bad. It is music that the common everyday working man can relate to. Many country songs are confessions; others are mere revelations.

If country music is a way of life for many in the south, it is also a journey. I know. It is a good and reliable companion that has traveled with me for more than 50 years.

> Bo Whaley, *The Official Redneck Handbook*, 1997. Reprinted by permission of Rutledge Hill Press, Nashville, Tennessee

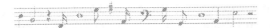

Science does a splendid job of magnifying the human voice, but it fails woefully with the voice of conscience.

If an opera cannot be played by an organ grinder, it is not going to achieve immortality.

> Thomas Beecham

A pessimist is a singer who gets depressed even when he sings "It's a Great Day."

Tenor: a high-pitched man's voice similar to a scream. Such singers often sing off-pitch, out-of-control and always sound like a cat that swallowed something down the wrong throat.

Burl Ives

Mary: "How would you describe a folksinger?"
Hary: "Let's see — hmmm, well, I'd say he was a baritone with a bad cold and a hair lip."

A soprano named Rugg married a man named Price. She was asked how the marriage was going and replied, " I parted with all my Ruggs for a good Price!"

Caruso, the great tenor, once asked a man why he always sang one tune. "I sing it because it haunts me," replied the singer.

"That's because you continually murder it," replied Caruso.

Octave: a distance of about eight note's if you include those semi-tones, and more than 27 if sung by a baritone.

How's this for caustic criticism: A newspaper printed a review of the opera *Il Trovatore*, saying of the Italian tenor: "Never before was *Trovatore* so ill."

Music Lover: A man, who upon hearing a beautiful soprano singing in the bathroom, puts his *ear* to the keyhole.

You ask me if I ever go to the opera? I sure do — whenever I need a rest and to sleep.

Contralto: A low form of music that women alone can sing.

Singing: Folks who go away to study music certainly should!

Q: "How many contraltos does it take to change a light bulb?"
A: "None. She gives that responsibility to her accompanist."

Applause is a receipt — not a note of demand!

"My voice held the audience open-mouthed. They all yawned at once."

An opera is a performance where the tenor gets stabbed in the back and instead of bleeding, he sings.

The greatest music lover of all is the woman who applauds her husband when he comes home at 3 A.M. singing.

You rarely hear sopranos practicing these days, except on TV and the radio.

Q: Why was the bass singer kicked out of his choir class?
A: Because he was always sliding into treble.

"That tenor is singing a truly difficult number, isn't he?"
"You bet. And I wish to God it were impossible!"

Voice floating out of the opera singer's dressing room: "I'm *not* conceited, although gosh knows I have every reason to be!"

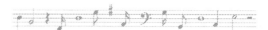

Quartet: a musical combination where three out of four think the other three can't sing.

After the concert in which the coloratura soprano had performed long and loud, a patron was heard to say: "That soprano should be charged with mutiny on the high C's."

A folk song is like a woman: You can recognize one, but you can't explain it.

We must believe in luck, for how else can we explain the success of those we don't like?

Jean Cocteau (1889-1963)

A record that seems never to be broken is the one the neighbors play after midnight.

Sign on a music store's delivery truck: "Drive with caution. We're all out of harps!"

The trouble with much of modern music is that you can't tell when the record is worn out.

In show business it's the box office that matters and not the applause.

Most show girls are remarkably lovely. It's sad to think that twenty years from now they'll be five years older.

Still another critic wrote about a Broadway musical: "I have criticized everything but the bowed legs of the chorus girls and nature anticipated me there."

A famous composer admits that "Few of our modern songs will live." And yet there are still critics who still dare to say: "We have so little to be thankful for!"

Show me a guy afraid of Christmas and I'll show you a *Noel* coward.

A primary factor in having a long run for a musical comedy is that there will be plenty of good legs in it.

Musician: a person who earns his livelihood by playing around.

Did you hear of the man who was going to write the best-ever drinking song? Well, he failed because he couldn't get past the first two bars.

The old popular songs are best, especially those that we don't sing anymore.

Consider this wise and witty saying from the down-home folks of Vermont: "Moonlight and Roses is a good subject for a song, but moonlight and a good ear of corn does much more for the stomach!"

Taxpayer's Anthem: "My Country, Tis Not Free."

"Aha! Just what I always suspected!"

Reprinted with permission of
The Saturday Evening Post Society

CHAPTER 5

Jazz, Popular and Country Music

These rock singers are really youngsters. The other night I asked one of them to autograph my program, and he did — in crayon!

After a rock concert, I went backstage and told them. "You guys have swell voices. You really should create a bar-bershop quartet."
They asked, "What's that?"
I asked, "Do you mean quartet?"
They replied, "No, barbershop."

Musical rap: Audible graffiti

The next door neighbor's little boy knocked on the door and said, "My daddy wants to know if you'll lend him your boom box tonight."
"Sure. Is he having a party?"
"No, he just wants a good night's sleep."

Good music is the kind we enjoyed when we were kids. *Bad* music is the kind today's kids like.

At a production of *My Fair Lady*, the two women sat in the audience, an empty seat between them. One said, "I waited eight months for my ticket."

"So did I," said the other.

"It's a shame — this empty seat," said the first.

"Oh, it's mine," said the other, "It was my husband's, but he died."

"Why didn't you bring a friend?" the other asked.

"Oh no," the other replied, shaking her head. "They're at the funeral."

© Field Enterprises, Inc., 1975

"You know Orville hates 'Tiger Rag!' especially during his nap."

Makin' Whoopee

Gus Kahn
1886-1941

Every time I hear that march from *Lohengrin*,
I am glad I'm on the outside looking in,
I have heard a lot of married people talk,
And I know that marriage is a long, long walk,

To some people weddings mean romance,
But I prefer a picnic or a dance.

Another bride, another June,
Another sunny honeymoon,
Another season, another reason,
For makin' whoopee!
A lot of shoes, a lot of rice,
The groom is nervous, he answers twice,
It's really killing that he's so willing
To make some whoopee!

Picture a little love-nest,
Down where the roses cling,
Picture the same sweet love-nest,
Think what a year can bring.
He's washing dishes and baby clothes,
He's so ambitious, he even sews.
But don't forget, folks,
That's what you get, folks,
For makin' whoopee!

Down through the countless ages
You'll find it everywhere,
Somebody makes good wages,
Somebody wants her share.
She calls him toodles, and rolls her eyes,
She makes him strudles, and bakes him pies,
What is it all for?
It's so he'll fall for
Makin' whoopee!

Another year, or maybe less,
What's this I hear, well can't you guess?
She feels neglected and he's suspected
Of makin' whoopee.
She sits alone most every night,
He doesn't phone or even write.
He says he's busy but she says "Is he?
He's makin' whoopee."
He doesn't make much money,

Five thousand dollars per,
Some judge who thinks he's funny
Says, "You pay six to her."
He says, "Now judge suppose I fail?"
The judge says, "Bud, right into jail,
You'd better keep her, you'll find it cheaper
Than makin' whoopee."

The head of that country music band is so conceited that every time he hears a clap of thunder, he goes to the window and takes a bow.

A New York City showgirl covered in a new mink coat encountered some old friends who complimented her on her new fur. "Oh this," she said coyly, shrugging her shoulders. "I got it for a mere song."

"Song?" repeated her friend. "It looks more like an overture to me!"

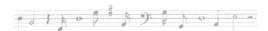

"What makes you think you're capable of leading a swing band?"

"Well, I'm recovering from a nervous breakdown, was an artilleryman during the war, and I live next door to a family with twelve kids."

Jimmy Durante, the late great comedian, claims an uncle who can play two songs at the same time. "With the left side of his mouth," said Jimmy, "he plays 'Life Is Just a Bowl of Cherries.' With the right side, he plays, 'Don't Sit Under the Apple Tree.'

"And with the middle of his mouth, he blows out the seeds."

Definition of a Rhumba: A foxtrot with the backfield in motion.

"Why on earth did you request Melancholy Baby?"

Reprinted with permission of
The Saturday Evening Post Society

During World War II, a draftee was sent to Honolulu and was thrilled by the hula dancers he encountered there. He wrote to his father, "I got to tell you, pop...those girls sure know how to shake hay while the son pines!"

A composer of red-hot jazz music came rushing into the office of his agent yelling, "I've just finished a song that'll knock your eyes out, it's so good!"

The agent pointed to the patch over his eye, saying, "I already heard it."

The greatest and nicest thing about a popular song is that — well — it isn't very popular very long.

A cute young girl entered a music store and walked up to the counter where a clerk was sorting sheet music. "Pardon me," she began, "But have you, 'Kissed Me in the Park One Night?'"

The new clerk blushed and turned to the girl and replied, "S-sorry, miss, but I'm new and have worked here only one week."

Ad in a New York City newspaper: "For sale: My boy's collection of doo-wop and rock-and-roll records. If a fifteen-year-old's voice answers the phone, hang up and call back later."

Symphony of the Southland

A fella' can do two things with country music. He can listen to it, or he can dance to it. I well remember the first time I danced to it. The year was 1941.

Being the son of a preacher and raised in the shadow of the steeple, I never really had the chance to learn much about dancing as a youngster, but I did try. Peer pressure, you know.

I went to my first dance in Luvale, a small community located half way between Lumpkin and Columbus. The girl whose mama owned the only juke in town invited me.

I was fuzzy-faced and fourteen. I shaved three times before the dance that Saturday night, using my daddy's razor, and looked more like a butchered hog than a dashing troubadour bent on tripping the light fantastic. And you can accentuate the word *tripping*.

In preparation for my debut, I practiced all Saturday afternoon in front of the bathroom mirror, using a plunger for a partner. And I might add that the plunger was built better than most of the girls at the dance. Well, it really wasn't a dance. They didn't have dances in Luvale. It was a "daintz," and there's a definite difference, Delsey.

The music, always country, was provided by a juke box in the corner next to the drink box that featured such classics of the early 40's as "Down Yonder," "Walking the Floor Over You," "Have You Ever Been Lonely," "Soldier's Last Letter," "By The Light of the Silvery Moon," and "Wreck on the Highway."

In 1941 the songs went for a nickel each, six for a quarter. But the juke box had a sensitive spot that one of the boys knew about where if you tapped it just right the songs would keep coming.

I rode to the dance with my best friend, Dan Ford. He was a good dancer, but the girl he took to the dance moved around the floor like a petrified pine. Dan kept bribing me with R.C. Colas to dance with her so he could trip around the cornmeal-covered floor with Marie Parks, the Ginger Rogers of Luvale. Man, that girl could flat *dance*!

I gave Dan's date Kate a nickname that night that stuck with her right on through high school: "Plunger." And the last I heard of her she was operating a bulldozer in the Columbus area.

"Goose" Geeslin was at the dance, too. "Goose" was only slightly smaller than a water tank, and tough. They didn't nobody at Stewart County High School mess with "Goose," who had light red hair and an over-abundance of freckles all over. He weighed in at around 210, all muscle. No doubt about it, "Goose" Geeslin would cut you.

For most of the night "Goose" sat by the drink box and watched. He watched Marie Parks. She didn't take a dance step all night long that he didn't see. When she sat down, he zeroed in on her. "Goose" was sweet on Marie in his own way.

On into the night the juke was playing a soft, sweet tune, "By the Light of the Silvery Moon," and Goose was staring holes through Marie.

"Why don't you ask her to dance, Goose?" I asked him.

"Uh-uh. Can't do that," he said.

"Why not?"

"Jus' can't, that's all," he growled.

"Aw, go on an' ask her," I prodded.

"Nope. Can't do that for two reasons," he allowed. "If I ask her to daintz an' she says 'yes' I'll be in a mess, an' if she says 'no' I'll be in a mess."

"Why? What do you mean?"

"Well, it's like this," he said. "If she says 'yes,' I can't daintz. An' if she says 'no,' I'll more'n likely knock hell out of her!"

Going to my first dance at the ripe old age of fourteen was one thing, but going to a country music concert in 1984 at the ripe old age of 56 was another. I thoroughly enjoyed it, but what I saw that day was an eye-opener. The performing group was *Alabama*, the best in the business. Come with me, if you will, to the concert that was staged in the Macon Coliseum.

Is there life after *Alabama*? The devoted fans of the musical group, "Entertainers of the Year" in 1982 and 1983 by vote of the Country Music Association, aren't real sure. They think that when you die you go to Fort Payne, Alabama, home turf of the colorful and talented youngsters.

The drive to Macon was very pleasant, until I approached the Coliseum entrance. The line of cars resembled an automotive assembly plant. I by-passed the parking lot and managed to find a parking place somewhere in the vicinity of Atlanta, 89 miles away.

After a nice, but long, hike I entered the Coliseum and located my seat. A great seat. Nothing but the best. It was in the last row (row 50), about two steps removed from a concessions stand and behind a post. I could hear *Alabama*, but I couldn't see them. Of course, the people up near Atlanta where my car was parked could probably hear them, too. And I'm sure they had better seats.

With a 45-minute wait until the show was scheduled to start, I enjoyed watching the crowd file in. It consisted of long ones, short ones, skinny ones, fat ones, pretty ones, ugly ones, young ones, old ones — with one thing in common. They loved *Alabama*. And I saw more blue jeans than Levi Strauss, Gloria Vanderbilt, Calvin Klein, Lee, Chic, and Mr. Wrangler ever dreamed of. Tight? Friends and neighbors, most of the female jeans were Vidalia onion skin tight. One girl, about nineteen, was sporting a pair so tight that her appendectomy scar was plainly visible. If they had busted we'd have all been killed!

If there has ever been 10,000 country music lovers gathered together under one roof and ready to party, it was the Sunday afternoon throng in Macon Coliseum. You could feel it as the 3:00 P.M. starting time approached.

About 2:47 P.M. the hand-clapping began. This was followed by foot-stomping at 2:55. Then, the announcement came: "The start of the show has been changed to 3:15 to allow those trying to park additional time to get inside," the public address man said.

"Why the heck didn't they park up near Atlanta and walk, like I did?" I asked of no one in particular. And no one in particular answered. They were too busy clapping their hands and stomping their feet.

Shortly after 3:00 P.M., a young couple wearing blue jeans arrived and took their seats in front of me on row 49. The male was holding what appeared to be about a three-month-old baby boy, dressed out in a miniature *Alabama* T-shirt.

Once seated, the female reached into one of those carry-all bags, pulled out a baby bottle, and handed it to her husband, who was holding the baby. The little fan knew exactly what to do with it, and in a few minutes it was empty.

Of course, Daddy knew what to do. He placed the child's head on his shoulder and patted his back gently, then firmer. Baby came through with flying colors.

"Buuuuuuuurrrrppp!"

Did I say the crowd was in a party mood? You better

believe it, because when the baby boy burped three couples seated in the immediate vicinity got up and danced.

It was a dadgummed good concert. That *Alabama* can flat get it on.

Bo Whaley, *The Official Redneck Handbook*, 1997. Reprinted by permission of Rutledge Hill Press, Nashville, Tennessee

"This is hell for me. I used to be a rock star."

That eminent composer and band leader Duke Ellington, who understandably is not displeased when disciples refer to him as "The American Bach," often quotes that same Bach in his casual conversation. The Duke once was heard to remark, speaking about piano playing, "As Bach says, if you ain't got a left hand, you ain't worth a hoot in hell."

I had an awful dream last night — I dreamt that the guy who invented Muzac invented something else.

Perry Como asked Pearl Bailey, guest star on his TV show, whether she ever sang for the pleasure of singing. She replied, "Well, if you'll examine that musical scale, you'll find it begins and ends with 'dough.'"

Musical Message

Yuppies reached bliss
With the Beatles and Kiss,
But I think they oughter
Learn Gershwin and Porter.

> Robert Gordon
> *Wall Street Journal*

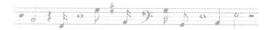

Old songs will have to be modernized for the space age. So we suggest "Shine On Harvest Sputnik" or "By the Light of the Silvery Satellite."

A popular song is one that has the happy virtue of making all of us think we can sing.

"That friend of yours told me that he's had a tune running through his head all evening. Is he a musician?"

"Don't know about that. But I do know there's nothing in there to stop it."

"Did you know that bees — yes bees — love and compose music? Well, let me tell you, their most recent composition is: STINGIN' IN THE RAIN.

"And I tell you it isn't! Our song is Star Dust!"

Reprinted with permission of
The Saturday Evening Post Society

I am amazed at radio DJ's today. I am firmly convinced
that AM on my radio station stands for Absolute Moron. I will
not begin to tell you what FM stands for.

Jasper Carrott

My son loves cool music. I guess that's why he put his
stereo in the refrigerator.

Three farts and a raspberry orchestrated.

> British conductor, Sir John Barbirolli
> describing modern music (1890-1970)

Rock 'n roll music makes me long for the good old days of radio when all you got was static.

Symphonies stretch your soul, jazz tickles your muscles.

> Paul Whiteman

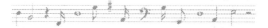

I'm the man who put unk in funk.

> American blues musician Muddy Waters (1914-1983)

Disc Jockey: A guy who lives on spins and needles.

Music is the language of the soul. Jazz must be the curse of words.

Theme song of the parachute corps: "It don't mean a thing if you don't pull that string."

People who like music with their meals should always eat soup.

Some conservatives say that the guy who invented the music named swing ought to.

I still believe in the future of love songs. After all, nobody has ever written a hit song about hate.

Richard Rogers 1971

When a new musical review appeared on Broadway, a particular critic didn't find it funny. He wrote: "I wouldn't leave a turn unstoned!"

Modern jazz is here to stay, but it can never replace the old-fashioned earache.

Playing 'Bop' is like Scrabble with all the vowels missing.

Duke Ellington

My girl used to sing with a band, but now she wears a little more.

In the old days, music had a nice upbeat to it. Today, the musicians sound beat-up!

There's a cogent rumor that next season there'll be a new musical and the setting is to be a steam bath. Title? "The Sauna Music."

Snore: "Sheet" music.

Perhaps the definitive statement on modern jazz was made on the evening a waiter tripped and dropped an entire trayload of dishes.

Eddie Condon was seated nearby and said, "None of that modern stuff in here!"

George Shearing, the blind pianist, tells the story of the time he put garlic on the reeds and mouthpieces of the horns in his orchestra.

The band leader began the beat with, "Now, fellows, one — two — three — four —" and all you could hear was "Ech-h-h! Gr-f-f-f!" and such sounds and coughing. Not a single note was heard.

Duke Ellington had been away from his orchestra for several weeks but was now back with them while they played a song from his movie, *Anatomy of a Murder*. Duke pointed at Paul Gonzales, telling him he should begin a solo for one of his *Anatomy* themes.

But Paul said his music was blank at that place.

"Ah, baby," said Duke, "That's where you begin on the adlibsaphone."

Dancing: Hugging set to music.

Practical dreamer: A person with an ear for music and a nose for lamb chops.

A recent musical comedy got this poisonous review: "I must admit that I saw the show under unfortunate circumstances — the curtain was up."

There are just two kinds of jazz: good and bad.

Eddie Condon

I prefer to eat in restaurants where they have music. The music makes me forget the awful food and food helps me forget the music.

Every time we hear a disc jockey playing the top ten popular tunes, we get the shakes thinking what the bottom ten must be like.

High school lad: "I'm looking for a new song. It goes zippity zappity, zoom-zoom-zoom."
"What are the words?"
"Those ARE the words, dummy!"

Rock music isn't dead — it's always smelled that way.

I had an unusual experience today. I had sent to our local radio station for an advertised item, "Oldies But Goodies," and they sent me a photograph of Mae West.

Pete Agar created a three-piece combo consisting of an organ, a cup and a monkey.

Farmer Jenkins had read that music affects the milk flow of cows, and that certain music can radically increase the flow. So one morning he took his guitar to the milk shed and began to play "There'll Be a Hot Time in the Old Town Tonight!"

Six of his cows began to kick and to bellow as he played the tune and finally they gored Jenkins and kicked his banjo into the hay loft. And do you know that to this very day there has never been a music critic who showed a more accurate judgement of that sort of music!

Jazz band director: A fellow who makes you dance to his music.

Just show me an adult who can grin through a rock 'n roll concert and I'll show you a person with weak batteries in his hearing aid!

Away with the music of Broadway,
Be off with your Irving Berlin,
Oh, I give no quarter
To Kern or Cole Porter,
And Gershwin keeps pounding on tin.
How can I be civil
While hearing this drivil,
It's strictly for night-clubbing souses.
Oh, give me the free 'n' easy
Waltz that is Viennesy
And,
Go tell the band
If they want a hand,
The waltz must be Strauss's.

George and Ira Gershwin
"By Strauss," song from *The Show Is On,* 1936

Pop music is the classical music of now.

Paul McCartney

Epitaph for a tombstone of a cool musician: "Man, this cat is really gone."

Reprinted with permission from
More Playboy's Party Jokes, 1965

Bert: "Did you know that I've taken up jazz song writing for a career?"
Ernie: "Great! Sold anything yet?"
Bert: "Yep! My watch, saxophone and — my topcoat!"

The budding composer sent words and music to a Broadway producer and asked, "Please, let me know at once if you can use it for I have other irons in the fire."
The producer wrote back, "Remove irons and insert music."

Two ladies were discussing their sons:
Mrs. J.: "My son has asked a lovely girl to marry him. He told her that he's near the top of TV brass."
Mrs. Y.: "Wait'll she finds out he plays trombone in the TV orchestra!"

Larry: "Isn't that a popular song he's singing up there?"
Mary: "It sure was before he sang it!"

"That's a wonderful rendition of 'Another Day Older and Deeper in Debt' — but loan denied."

You tell 'em, Tin Pan. It's right up your alley!

The kids today are right about the music their parents listened to. Most of it was poor trash. The parents are right about what their young listen to. Most of it is poor trash too.

Gene Lees
"Rock" High Fidelity, 1967

A publisher of popular music was heard judging a piece given him for publication: "Those are the countriest lyrics I've ever heard! And so damned sentimental. Beside that, the thing repeats itself with an absolutely uninspired lyric. Phooie! Y'know what — I think we got a hit on our hands!"

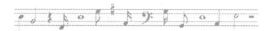

Producer: "What genre of stage show would you choose if the setting was a western ranch?"
Singer: "A moosical, of course."

"The big band era never ends, jam sessions last forever and gigs are eternal."

Jazz is the kind of music that we keep thinkin'll turn into a tune.

Frank McKinney Hubbard
1868-1930

I hate music, especially when it's played.

Jimmy Durante
1893-1980

Success in Music City U.S.A.

My friend Robbie Nell Bell recently quit her waitress job at Mel's Juke, had the water pump fixed on her '73 Ford, and moved to Nashville. She's taken up writin' country songs full time.

She called (collect) from Nashville one Saturday night after the Grand Ole Opry from a Nashville spot called the Ace of Spades.

"How in the world are you, Robbie Nell?" I asked.

"Fine, Chief, jus' fine," she said. "Writin' country songs an' makin' money faster'n a bootlegger. Eventhink' 'bout gittin' married agin soon's my boyfriend, Roy, gits his d'vorce from that ol' Margie."

"Well, congratulations. What took you to Nashville?" I asked.

"Y'member that song I wrote that Bobby an' th' Rattlesnakes recorded in Waycross 'bout two years ago, "Pap Died and Mama Cried, 'Cause the Insurance Had Done Lapsed?"

"Right, I remember. A real tear-jerker," I said.

"Wail, that's whut started th' whole thaing," she said. Roy, tha's my boyfriend, heard it an' his band, Roy's Ramblers, recorded it. Roy done th' saingin', naturally, an' it became a big hit. So now, I write 'em an' Roy saings 'em. He gives me seven dollars f'r ever one I write."

"I'm proud of you. Have you written very many?" I asked.

"Shoot I reckon! A whole 'baccer sheet full," she bellowed, "I had a real big 'un right after Thanksgiving las' year when my brother's wife run off with th' Roto-Rooter man."

"What was the name of it?"

"You mean you ain't heard it? It's called, 'I Stuffed Her Turkey and She Cooked My Goose.'" "I tell you what, I'll jus' send all of 'em down to you an' you can be my Georgia agent. How 'bout that?"

"Great! Send 'em on down. You have lots of fans in this area.," I told her.

I'm not sure you're ready for this, but here is the list of songs written by Robbie Nell Bail, that arrived in the morning mail:

"When I'm Alone I'm in Bad Company"

"A Sad Song Don't Care Whose Heart It Breaks"

"I Wouldn't Take Her to a Dogfight, But I Know She'd Win if I Did"

"I May Fall Again, But I'll Never Get Up This Slow"

"You're the Busiest Memory in Town"

"Your Face is Familiar, But I Forget Your Name"

"You Don't Have to Go Home, Baby, But You Can't Stay Here"

"It's Easy to Find an Unhappy Woman Till I Start Looking for Mine"

"The More I Think of You, the Less I Think of Me"

"Don't Cry Down My Back, Baby, You Might Rust My Spurs"

"I Can't Afford to Half My Half Again"

"The Bridge Washed Out, I Can't Swim, and My Baby's on the Other Side of the River"

"Forever, for Us, Wasn't Nearly as Long as We Planned On"

"I Got to Her House Just in Time to be Late"

"I'm Afraid to Come Home Early Without Warning Her First"

"My Wife Ran Off with My Best Friend — And I Sure Do Miss Him"

"Send Her a Dozen Roses, and Pour Four for Me"

"He's Walking in My Tracks, But He Can't Fill My Shoes"

"She's Gone, and She Took Everything but the Blame"

"I Can't Believe I Gave Up 'Good Mornin' Darling' and 'We Love You Daddy,' for This"

"I'd Rather Be Picked Up Here Than to Be Put Down Home"

"When the Phone Don't Ring, You'll Know It's Me That Ain't Calling"

148

"If You Want to Keep the Beer Real Cold, Put It Next to My Ex-Wife's Heart"

"I Need Somebody Bad Tonight 'Cause I just Lost Somebody Good Today"

"The Score Is: Liars One — Believers Zero"

"I'm Ashamed to Be Here, but Not Ashamed Enough to Leave"

"How Can Six-year-old Whiskey Beat a Thirty-two-year-old Man?"

"She's Waiting on Tables While Waiting for the Tables to Turn"

"Now That She's Got Me Where She Wants Me, She Don't Want Me"

"I Can't Even Do Wrong Right No More"

"The Devil Is a Woman in a Short Red Dress"

"She Ain't Much to See, But She Looks Good Through the Bottom of a Glass"

"I Done 'Bout Lived Myself to Death"

"It's Bad When You Get Caught with the Goods"

"Remember to Remind Me I'm Leaving"

"It Took a Hell of a Man to Take My Ann, But it Sure
Didn't Take Him Long to Do It"
"Them What Ain't Got Can't Lose"
"I'm Sick and Tired of Waking Up Sick and Tired"

Bo Whaley, *The Official Redneck
Handbook*, 1997. Reprinted by
permission of Rutledge Hill Press,
Nashville, Tennessee

"Sure, we can give it a tune-up. You want classical, pop or country?"

Th' Jazz Orchestra Menace
By Abe Martin

A census of th' jazz orchestras throughout th' United States has jest been completed an' the' figures are staggerin'. Unless some vigorous action is taken t' stem th' tide o' youth in th' direction o' dance orchestras, our whole economic structure must tumble, t' say nothin' o' th' regular army.

Th' exodus o' young men from th' useful walks o' life t' th' saxophone alone mounts well int' th' hundreds o' thousan's, while those who are devotin' th' golden, habit formin' years of ther lives t' trombones an' trap drums may easily be surmised, since wherever ther's a saxophone th' drums an' trombone are hard by.

Employers o' child labor are complainin' bitterly, while parents who wish t' make dentists an' plasterers o' ther sons are wringin' ther hands.

An' this present day craze among boys t' join slap bang orchestras is drivin' our girls int' th' professions. Instead o' prowlin' about durin' th' long summer evenin's with girls on ther arms, fully eighty per cent of our boys may be seen dartin' here an' there carryin' bass drums, fiddle boxes an' horns.

An' what kind o' music are they makin'? We saw a fine promisin' lookin' boy buyin' a stiff hat fer his trombone th' other day with money his father had given him, not fer mowin' th' lawn or washin' th' car, but jest out o' th' goodness of his heart. We know his dad an' he's a fine, conscientious cement mixer an' wears a cap daily an' Sunday.

The saxophone is an ole time musical instrument, an' fer many years, or up t' th' time jazz got prominent, it had no standin' whatever in decent, ear–respectin' musical organizations, but t'day its low, degradin' notes predominate at all dances. Wealthy saxophone manufacturers spend ther time in Europe, while retailers in saxophones are buyin' costly estates in Californy.

We don' t know how true it is, but we've heard that these jazz orchestra boys make three dollars an hour while they last. But what o' th' future years, but what o' th' day o' reckonin' when jazz bites th' dust, when these boys are tossed int' th' arena o' life with nothin' t' commend 'em but an ear fer noise? Gittin' stuck on a musical instrument is different from any other infatuation. We kin have most any other kind of a hobby an' still study law, or medicine, or learn a trade, but becomin' endeared t' a musical instrument destroys th' desire fer all other earthly things.

"Great location."

© 1998 Jonny Hawkins

"Everything must die, son, except of course, rock and roll."

CHAPTER SIX

Percussion

TYMPANUM

The Vibrant Bowl, the TYMPANUM,
(It's also called a Kettle drum)
However lightly we may treat it,
For solid skill, it's hard to beat it.
A tympanist to make it clear
Must play it both by hand and ear,
Manipulating gadgets which
Will bring it smartly up to pitch'
Then, pots encircling him about,
He stands prepared to dish it out,
And from his tubs the flavor floats
Of ticked beats and hot rolled notes
As from these mammoth soup tureens
Come thunder storms and battle scenes
A sweet existence we presume,
This life of everlasting boom.

Laurence McKinney, *People of Note*
(Out of print for nearly 30 years, will be
re-released in 1999. If you can't locate
a copy, try Amazon.com on the internet)

We have recently been blessed by a new Latin American-Japanese version of our national anthem. It's composed by Jose Kenyusi.

"What ever happened to the big guy who used to play base drum in your marching band?" a patron asked the band director.

"Oh, about four months ago he quit us," was the reply.

"What a shame. I thought he was terrific. What happened?"

"He was always overweight, but recently he got so darned fat that when he marched with the band, he couldn't hit the drum on the skin, only on the rim."

"Did you have to ask him to play a Sousa march?"

Definition of a kettle drum: Don't be fooled by the title, "Kettle Drum," because they aren't much use in boiling water for tea or coffee. They once were used to simulate cannon in warfare and, even, thunder. But now they are more often used to imitate the more nasty bodily functions. But they are great as a base for playing checkers.

Noise: Sometimes called "music"

Charles Dickens commented on a certain person that he was "dumb as a drum with a hole in it, Sir."

"Why couldn't he have just taken up the guitar or the fiddle, like everybody else?"

A peculiar fellow named Kroch
Would beat the base drum with his (ahem) sock.
Without exception he could play any selection
From Johann Sebastian Bach.

First Child: "What did you get for Christmas?"
Second Child: "I got a wonderful set of drums. Best present I ever got."
First Child: "Really? Why?"
Second Child: "Because Dad gives me five bucks a week not to play them."

Triangle: A small triangular–shaped metallic oddity used by drummers to vex the rest of the players. It is also a kind of romance not to be undertaken by musicians who want to avoid embarrassment, heartache and financial or legal problems.

"He always lets us know when he's hungry."

He wasn't the smartest drummer in the town. When we asked him to spell Mississippi he asked, "Do you mean the state or the river?"

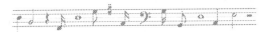

Q: Why does an army band drummer have a teensy weensie bit more brains than the captain's horse?
A: So he doesn't do as horses do all over the parade grounds.

Q: What does it tell you when you see a drummer drooling out of both sides of his mouth?
A: That you are on a level stage.

"What's better than a busted drum?"
"I don't know. Tell me!"
"Nothing. It's unbeatable!"

"Were you able to wake Daddy up?"

Teacher: "Can you give us a description of the drum?"

Student: "OK, here goes. It's an instrument you can't beat for noise."

Jim: "That drum majorette is sure cute. I'd like to take her out. Do you know her room number?"

Tim: "Sure do. It's Suite 16."

A humdrummer: An uninspired percussionist.

"Cut that out!"

If thine enemy offend thee, give his kid a drum and you'll be even!

Josh Billings
1818-1885

What's the difference between a kettle drum and a lawn mower?

The neighbor gets mad if you don't return the lawn mower.

A kettle drummer who wants to be a cymbalist in the worst way.

CHAPTER SEVEN

Symphonies, Composers and Conductors

The musician: A person who makes a living by playing around. A man who plays when he works and works when he plays.

I kissed my girl and smoked my first cigarette on the same day. I have not had time for tobacco since.

Artur Toscanini
(1867-1957)

Listening to the *Fifth Symphony* of Ralph Vaughn Williams is like staring at a cow for 45 minutes.

Aaron Copeland
(1900-1988)

First you go out and buy a stick — it's called a baton — about this long. Then you get some music, you get musicians together, you give them this music, you stand in front of them with the stick in your right hand, you go like this, and a mysterious thing happens: the musicians begin to play. Now, once the musicians are playing there are only two things you must remember, but they are very important: you must not disturb the musicians while they are playing, and second, when the musicians have stopped playing you must stop conducting.

Sigmund Romberg
Friendly Advice by Jon Winokur

"Thought you said we were going to a hillbilly mountaineers' concert!"

Rossini would have been a great composer if his teacher had spanked him enough on his backside.

Ludwig Van Beethoven
(1770-1827)

The youth looked nervous. "Well — er — I got a song here," he began, "that I wrote and I want you to publish it. Shall I sing it?"

"Oh, yes; let's hear it!" said the publisher. And the youth stood up and burst forth valiantly.

When the song was finished the publisher sat very still and said nothing.

"Well," the young man asked, impatiently, "What do I get for it?"

"Don't ask me," replied the publisher, with an air of resignation, "I'm the publisher, not the circuit judge!"

Larry: "Don't you simply hate people who talk behind your back?"
Lulu: "I certainly do — especially at the symphony concert."

There are more bad musicians than there is bad music.

Isaac Stern

At the first performance of George Antheil's ultra-modernistic *Ballet Mécanique*, the orchestra contained eight grand pianos, seven xylophones, a fire-alarm siren, an airplane propeller and several automobile horns. As the music mounted in volume the audience became restless and continued to grow fidgety and excited. Finally after ten minutes of the composition, a man in the front row raised a white handkerchief tied to his cane and the audience burst into laughter.

There's only one woman I know of who could never be a symphony conductor — and that woman is Venus de Milo.

Margaret Hillis
1921

Famous novelist William Styron's four-year-old daughter once fancied herself a connoisseur of fine music. She was listening intently to Leonard Bernstein leading his orchestra on TV one morning when her father inquired, "Do you know what they're playing?" The daughter answered haughtily, "I'm quite sure, it's one of those symphonies by Boat-Haven."

Mrs. Bernbaum came uptown for her first symphony concert at Carnegie Hall. Her neighbors heard about nothing else the next afternoon. "Such an experience," she sighed blissfully.

Her friend asked her which piece she had enjoyed the most.

"Let me see now," she mused. "I guess best I liked Tchaikovsky's Symphony — if you'll pardon the expression — No. 2."

Many a musician who plays Beethoven, should play poker.

Musician: A person who earns his living by playing around.

To those who love to talk, the symphony concert is that which surrounds the intermission.

Ned Roram
(1923-1974)

We were giving a concert. After the last strains of Handel's "Largo" floated out, a fat, motherly woman came up to me and asked, "Will you please play Handel's 'Largo'?"

"Ma'am, we've just finished playing it," I replied.

The fat lady went back in her chair, saying, "Oh, I wish I'd known that. It's my favorite piece. I love it best of all."

"Could I see your seat stubs, please?"

You tell me he is a musician. I knew that, but tell me what he does for a living?

Orchestra: The group that occurs because musicians have learned that there is safety in numbers. Can be differentiated from a mob because mobs use sticks and stones while the orchestra uses weapons such as tubas and cellos and oboes and clarinets.

I know only two kinds of audiences — one coughing and one not coughing.

Arthur Schnabel
(1882-1951)

Italian composer, Rossini, who enjoyed night life, was once told by his doctor: "Your trouble stems from wine, women and song."

"I don't especially need the songs," volunteered Rossini, "as I compose my own."

"Which of the other two are you prepared to drop?" asked the doctor.

"That," replied Rossini, "depends altogether on the vintage."

Variation: The sort of music that composers do when they cannot make up their minds.

Why are the hearts of conductors so much in demand for heart transplants?

Because they are in pristine, almost unused condition.

After the concert, the audience applauded uproariously. But even more enthusiastic was the clapping of the two ushers.

One seated attendee whispered to his partner: "Those two ushers really did appreciate this concert — just listen to their applause!"

Then the seated person heard one of the ushers whisper to the other, "Keep it up, Joe, just two more minutes and we get overtime."

When George Gershwin died, a man wrote a eulogy in his honor. He asked Gershwin's friend, Oscar Levant, if he would agree to hear the tribute. The man read the eulogy to Levant and then waited for his oponion. He soon got it. Levant said, "I think it would have been better if you had died and Gershwin had written your eulogy."

De Pachman discovered he'd mislaid his false teeth. A lover of puns, he told a friend: "Now my Bach is worse than my bite."

His Better Half

Professor Schultz was the star of the Muenchen Annual Concert. Before he put the cornet to his lips, he announced: "I vill now play it, the classical piece, 'Poet and Peasant'."

And with that, he went to work on the cornet. When he had finished, a heckler cried, "That was terrible — what's the name of that piece?" Professor Schultz, burned up, replied, "Don't care vat came out — I blew in 'Poet and Peasant'."

Good musicians execute their music. Bad musicians murder it.

Musical snob: A person who believes he knows far more about music than we do.

Conductors should give suggestions through movement directed to the orchestra and not choreography to the audience.

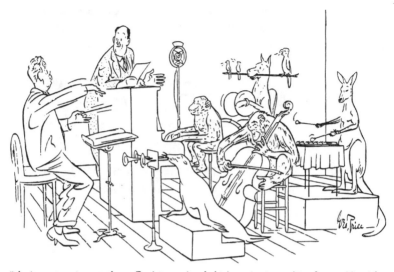

"You've got a nice act there, Fredricson, but I think you're just asking for trouble with the musician's union."

Reprinted with permission of
The Saturday Evening Post Society

An efficiency authority was hired to evaluate a famous American symphony. He submitted this report to the board of directors of the symphony:

For long periods of time, the four clarinet players have little to do. Their number could be vitally reduced and the work passed to more members of the orchestra, thus more efficiently using the staff. At one time, all ten violinists were playing the same notes, indicating unnecessary duplication of effort. Much could be gained by having them play different notes or be silent.

A further waste seems to be the repeating by the brass of notes already played by the strings.

We estimate that if all duplicate passages in the works were eliminated that the entire concert of three hours might be shortened to twenty minutes at a considerable saving of expenses and the total elimination of intermissions.

Never blow your own horn unless you're in an orchestra.

There are two golden rules for an orchestra: They must begin together and end together; the public doesn't give a damn what goes on in between.

Thomas Beecham

The trouble with opera in the United States is that it is like having to sell caviar to a hamburger-eating country.

Helen Traubel

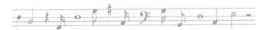

Both teachers and parents have their problems with teen-agers. Harold Dunn, for instance, who teaches music in Jefferson City, Missouri, offers these five excerpts from classroom essays:

Joseph Haydn was born 1732, and soon became the father of classical music. Later, at the age of twenty-eight, he got married. Haydn had a lot of will power. He died in 1809 and is still dead.

Bach was the most famous composer in the world and so was Handel. Handel was half German, half English, and half Alsatian. He was rather large.

Chopin had many fast friends. Among the fastest was Miss Sand.

Paganini was a famous fiddler. He fiddled with many of the greatest singers in Europe.

Requiems are usually played for sad occasions like funerals and marriages. Fugues are also popular. The most popular fugue was the one between the Hatfields and the McCoys.

The man who applauded at the end of the first movement of the symphony.

Q: Why did the bandleader refuse to go outside during an electrical storm?

A: Because he was such a great conductor.

SWEET MUSIC — Some of you will recall the opening day of the first Patrol School in the wooden barracks after World War II. It was a cold, rainy Sunday afternoon in February. The barracks had been brought from abandoned army camps and were partially heated by antiquated coal stoves. Between the barracks was a latrine with commodes and lavatories — all ready to go. Men had been working in three shifts round the clock laying the pipes to bring hot and cold water, but they had come only halfway to the building. I knew that if the prospective patrolmen had to go to the business instead of the commodes, and if they had no hot water to wash and shave with next morning, they wouldn't be there for another day. I was tired, sweaty, dirty and worried as I went home to clean up and dress up, and I was worried as I returned for the formal opening of the school after the evening meal.

Here was my greeting to the expectant rookies:

Gentlemen, I have heard Serge Koussevitzky lead the Boston Symphony Orchestra. I have heard Walter Damrosch lead the New York Philharmonic. I have heard Eugene Ormandy lead the Philadelphia Orchestra. But no one of these orchestras alone, nor all of their instruments together, ever made music as sweet to me as the sound of forty flushing commodes on a trial run as I came by the latrine building on my way to this opening ceremony.

> [Albert Coates, from manuscript of
> talk to law-enforcement officers.]
> *Tar Heel Laughter*
> edited by Richard Walzer
> University of North Carolina,1974

A prima dona's idea of a conceited person is anyone who doesn't have her in mind.

Making music is like making love; the act is always the same, but each time it's different.

> Arthur Rubenstein

The wife loved music but hubby hated it. Finally, she dragged him to Orchestra Hall to hear the symphony. But they didn't arrive in their seats until 10 p.m. After consulting the program, the wife whispered, "They're in the middle of Beethoven's Ninth Symphony."

Husband replied: "Thank heaven. I've missed the other eight of 'em."

Composers should write tunes that chauffeurs and errand boys can whistle.

Sir Thomas Beecham

Composers shouldn't think too much — it interferes with their plagiarism.

Howard Dietz

Q: Why did the conductor lug a baseball to the concert?
A: He wanted to have the right pitch.

Music is the refuge of souls ulcerated by happiness.

E. M. Cioran

Puns are not normally part of the music scene, but this one fits:

It seems that a certain conductor who had murdered most of the compositions he had directed, was sentenced to be electrocuted for his criminal treatment of music. He was strapped into the chair, the current was turned on, but he did not die. Why? It was discovered that electricity could not kill the man because — because he was such a poor conductor!

I have been told that Wagner's music is better than it sounds.

Bill Nye

After silence, that which comes nearest to expressing the inexpressible, is music.

Aldous Huxley

Johannes Brahms was strolling with a friend along a Vienna boulevard when they came to a house with a commemorative plaque on it. "The day following my death," said Brahms, "they'll put up a sign in front of my house, just like this one."

"Of course," remarked his friend, "and it'll read 'House To Let.'"

Nobody really sings in an opera — they just make noises.

Amelita Galli-Curci

John Barbirolli, the famous conductor, once remarked to his musicians: "Ladies and Gentlemen, that passage should sound like the night! But you make it sound like the morning after."

The world rarely recognizes a composer until after his death — and then he's safe.

The most important advantage one has as a conductor is that one doesn't have to face the audience.

During his first tour of the United States, Igor Stravinsky's command of English was poor. During the concert he directed, the oboe player made the same mistake time after time and yet Stravinsky never bawled the musician out.

Later a friend complimented him on his great self-control. Stravinsky responded: "I don't speak English well, as you know, but you should have heard what I called him under my breath in Russian!"

If you think you're boring your audience, go slower not faster.

Gustav Mahler

After one of the Boston Symphony's performances in Symphony Hall, an excited admirer swept backstage to conductor Serge Koussevitzky's dressing room. "Maestro!" she cried. "Maestro, you play so wonderfully! You — you are simply God!"

Koussevitzky turned to the woman and, with a perfectly humble face, said: "Yes, madom — and *soch* a responsibility."

Musical people always want one to be perfectly dumb at the very moment when one is longing to be absolutely deaf.

Oscar Wilde

A symphony orchestra was playing Beethoven's *Leonore* overture, the two climaxes of which are followed by a trumpet passage offstage.

The first climax was met and played beautifully but there was no sound from the trumpet offstage. The second time for the trumpet passage came and went — no trumpet!

Finished with the overture, the conductor rushed offstage and met the trumpeter in heated argument with the house fireman.

"I keep telling you," the fireman said, "that you can't play that thing back here. You keep asking me why and I keep telling you that there is a concert going on out on that stage!"

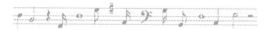

Pianist Oscar Levant once talked himself out of a speeding ticket by explaining to the policeman that he had been listening to a concert on his car radio. "You can't possibly hear the last movement of Beethoven's Seventh, and go slow," he said.

Bach was the most famous of all composers — and so was Handel.

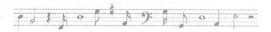

Q: Why did the conductor put a clock in full view of the orchestra?

A: Because he wanted to be certain that the orchestra kept proper time.

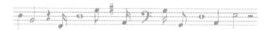

The symphony concert was full of surprises. I just wish it had been full of talents.

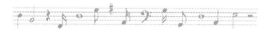

Harry: "Did that new symphony have a pleasing ending?"

Mary: "You bet it did! Everyone was pleased when it was over."

Question: "Why did the music students hate their teacher?"

Answer: "She was just too hot-tempoed."

Conductors must give unmistakable and suggestive signals to the orchestra—not choreography to the audience.

George Szell

Mrs. Jones: "I saw you at the concert last night. Didn't you think the music heavenly?"

Mrs. Bones: "Not exactly. I thought of it as from the other direction."

Q: "If a conductor and a bass player are standing on the end of a pier, which do you push in first?"

A: "The conductor. Always put business before pleasure."

What I like best about music is the women who listen to it.

Jules Goncourt (1830-1870)

Too many pieces (of music) finish too long after the end.

Igor Stravinsky

Von Bulow was going downstairs when he bumped into a stranger on the way.

"Jerk! Ass!" gritted the man.
"Charmed," Bulow replied. "And my name is Bulow."

One time, George Gershwin invited his friends to his home and gave a long performance of his own works accompanied by extended talk on his experiences, hopes, and ideals. After the performance. Oscar Levant asked him: "So tell us, George, if you had it to do all over again, would you still fall in love with yourself?"

The great conductor Arturo Toscanini was leading the orchestra in the performance of Debussy's *La Mer*. He was seeking a spiritual effect in one of the more ethereal passages but his English was not good enough to explain to the orchestra what he wanted. So he took out a white silk handkerchief and threw it into the air and it floated down softly and gently.

The players watched fascinated by the soft, sensuous flow of the fabric to the floor.

"Now!" exclaimed Toscanini. "Play it like that."

Teacher: "Can you name the famous vampire composer?"
Student: "Sure. Bathoven."

Bernie: "I play by ear."
Ernie: "I listen the exact same way!"

In a review of one of Marc Biltzstein's works, always radical and dissonant, a reviewer wrote: "His music is full of Donner and Blitzstein."

A little boy was at the concert with his mother when the lad noticed that, while the conductor had a huge beard, he was almost totally bald. He turned to his mother and whispered: "Mom, why doesn't that conductor have his hair grow in the right spot?"

A famous pianist finished his concerto and then appeared arm-in-arm with the conductor to take the audience's accolades. One patron remarked: "That's the only time tonight they've been together."

   Moisha Rabinovoff began his musical education almost
before he could talk. For over twenty years, he studied in
several conservatories. Then he played in concerts in major
European capitals — London, Vienna, Rome, Paris. Finally,
in New York, he played under Leopold Stokowski. During the
first rehearsal, playing with Stokowski, the great conductor
noticed he had a sour-puss look on his face.
   "Ha!" he thought. "This guy is a grump!"
   "Why have you got that grumpy look on your face?"
Stokowski asked. "Don't you like me?"
   "It's not that," answered Rabinovoff.
   "Maybe you don't like the other musicians?"
   "No, it isn't that."
   "Well, maybe you don't like the piece we're playing?"
   "No, it's not that, either."
   "Well, maybe you don't like the piece we're playing?"
   "No, it's not that, either."
   "Maybe you don't like this concert hall?"
   "That isn't it."
   "Well, there has got to be *something* wrong. What is it?"
   "*I just don't like music!*" moaned Rabinovoff.

   A famous portrait of Stravinsky is composed of a line
drawing by Picasso. Stravinsky was held for a time by
authorities at the Italian border because they figured this
drawing was a map of Italy's secret military installations!

I write music as a sow piddles.
                    Wolfgang Amadeus Mozart (1756-1791)

   Remember that nobody will ever get ahead of you as
long as he is kicking you in the pants.
                    Walter Winchell (1893-1964)

All the inspiration I ever needed was a phone call from a producer.

Cole Porter (1893-1964)

I know his mother only by correspondence, and one cannot arrange that sort of thing by correspondence. (On rumors that he was the father of pianist Franz Servais)

Franz Liszt (1811-1886)

After the performance of Shostakovich's *Seventh Symphony*, one critic wrote: "For Shostakovich, life begins at forte!"

Policeman: "How do you manage to get a symphony conductor down from a tree?"

Musician: "Cut the rope above the noose."

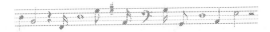

A certain composer known not only for his work but also his stinginess with money gave a dinner party after the performance of one of his works. Those invited were amazed that this skinflint of a man would not only give a party for others but would give such a lavish one. However, their amazement was entirely muted and changed into anger when, after dinner, each was presented a check for the feast.

Music teacher: "Can you give me a definition of an 'augmented fifth'?"

Student: "I'd describe it as a bottle of whiskey holding forty ounces."

Mine was the kind of piece in which nobody knew what was going on, including the conductor and the critics. Consequently, I got pretty good notices.

Liszt was a superb composer. The saying, "Last but not Liszt" came about when he failed to show up at a party.

After a wearing, bad rehearsal, Arturo Toscanni (1867-1957) said to the orchestra: "After I die, I shall return to the earth as the doorkeeper of a bordello and I won't let a single one of you in!"

Beethoven sounds to me like the upsetting of a bag of nails, with here and there, an also-dropped hammer.

John Ruskin (1819-1900)

MUSIC DEPT.

Sir Thomas Beecham's father burst into his room one day and exclaimed: "I've been spendin' lotsa dough on your education, Son, and now I want you to help me in my business. Do something musical for Beecham's pills."

After his father had left, the son began to do some thinking and finally resolved to go through the company's annual and reports and adapt some of it to poetry. Here's one of his poems:

Hark! The herald angels sing!
Beecham's pills are just the thing,
Two for a woman, one for a child —
Peace on earth and mercy mild!

Charles Baudelaire (1821-1867) remarked about music that he liked: "The music I prefer is that of a cat hung up by its tail outside a window and trying to stick to the pane of glass with its claws."

Professor: "What does a symphony orchestra require when it wants to play the *Minute Waltz* in five seconds?"
Student: "A lightning conductor!"

It is impossible to imagine Goethe or Beethoven being good at billiards or golf.

H. L. Mencken
(1880-1956)

An old, ill orchestra conductor played an ill-starred concert in America. After his awful performance at Carnegie Hall, the first violinist was asked, "What did he conduct tonight?" The violinist answered, "Lord knows what he conducted — but we played Tchaikovsky's Fifth."

In order to compose, all you need to do is to remember a tune that nobody else has thought of.

Robert Schuman (1810-1956)

The famous Philadelphia Symphony Orchestra once ran a contest for discovering local talent. Hundreds of applications were received, among which were these: A hurdy-gurdy player, a virtuoso on the spoon, a male coloratura soprano who had won first prize in a hog-calling contest, and a drum majorette who claimed to have "two pink dimpled knees."

Music is enjoyable if you listen to it with your eyes shut. But it is much more enjoyable if the people sitting near you listen with their mouths shut.

"I hate child prodigies!"

Cartoon Festival 1975
Reprinted with permission of The
Saturday Evening Post Society

Wagner's symphony music is better than it sounds.

Mark Twain
(1835-1910)

Classical music is the kind we keep thinking will turn into a tune.

Frank McKinney (Kim) Hubbard
(1868-1930)

Oscar Levant described Gershwin's music this way: "He has been disclosing musical secrets that have been known for over 400 years."

"How did you like my composition?" asked the aspiring composer of the music critic.

"I believe it will be performed long after Brahms, Beethoven and Bach are forgotten."

"Really? Do you think so?"

"I certainly do and not a moment before that!"

A critic is a man who knows the way but can't drive the car.

Kenneth Tynan (1927-1980)

Every time I look at you, I get a fierce desire to be lonesome.

Oscar Levant (1906-1972)

In a small Kansas town in the early years of this century, a symphony orchestra played Boccherini's *Minuet* and did an excellent job of it. When they finished the symphony, one music lover told the conductor that what had impressed him the most was that the musicians had all turned over the leafs of their music *at the same time.*

Don: "Why couldn't Mozart find his teacher?"
Joan: "Because he was Hayden!"

An Italian musician's son, recently having arrived in this country, was the only lad in his class who identified a selection played by the symphony orchestra. The composer was Pagannini and the teacher was delighted that the boy had properly identified the music.

"Your father's training, no doubt," beamed the teacher. "No seea my padre for seex years," the lad replied. "I reada da name offa da music."

The instructor looked at the music and saw "page 9"!

The conductor of the Cleveland Symphony Orchestra was given a terrible review in the major newspaper of that city. The conductor was not only furious at the review, but could hardly sleep. So he wrote the editor of the paper: "I am now just in the process of writing you about your review of my concert last night and I have before me your criticism. Soon — very soon — I'll have it in back of me!"

A well-known music critic ate much too heavily before rushing to the auditorium to hear a new symphony he was to review. At the end of the first act, he belched loudly, not once but several times. A lady sitting in front of him turned and said, "Sir, would you mind waiting until you get to your office before writing your review!"

"Oh, you simply must go to the concert tonight. They're playing my favorite number — *This is the End*," composed by Saul Over.

Wife #1: "I must tell you, my husband simply hates symphony music. At the opening bar, he gets up and goes home."

Wife #2: "You're lucky. Mine comes home only after they *close* the bars."

Show me a guy who's fearful of Christmas and I'll show you a Noel Coward.

Molly: "I read the simply wonderful review the critic gave last night's concert."

Polly: "I, too, read it. But I had no idea we enjoyed it that much!"

An old story has it that a pedestrian stopped Jascha Heifitz on the street and asked: "Sir, can you tell me how to get to Carnegie Hall?"

Heifitz replied: "Practice!"

The high school orchestra's performance was the worst ever. Even the school principal, who knew nothing about music, realized that it was bad. So he asked the conductor: "What does the future, next year, look like?"

"Bad! Read bad! None of my players are graduating."

They told me the director of the symphony got too familiar with his pretty young students, and I found that to be true. When I went to his rehearsal the first time he put his hand on my most intimate part and I liked to never got my wallet back.

Leopold Stokowski was one of the first conductors in America to lead an orchestra without a score or baton. Many years ago, when viewed while conducting without score or baton, a sweet old lady remarked: "It's a shame he can't read music. Wouldn't he be dandy if he just knew how!"

First ghost: "Where did you go on your vacation?"
Second ghost: "To the New York Philharmonic Auditorium."
First ghost: "Good for you. That's my favorite haunt, too."

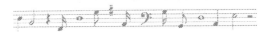

After the concert, a person was heard to say: "I've had a wonderful evening but this wasn't it."

If one hears bad music, it is one's duty to drown it in conversation.

Oscar Wilde
(1856-1900)

The culture-conscious young lady asked her friend, a professional musician, how to tell the difference between classical and some kinds of popular music.

"It's really quite simple, Jane," the musician replied. "When a piece seems every minute to be about to become a tune but never does, you can be positive that it's classical."

Show me a squirrel's nest and I'll show you "The Nutcracker Suite."

A young man asked Mozart how one went about writing a symphony.

"You are a very young man," Mozart replied. "Why don't you begin by composing a ballad?"

"But, Sir," replied the young fellow. "You composed symphonies when you were only ten years old."

"I know I did," replied Mozart. "But I didn't ask 'how'."

A patron at the concert was laying across four seats, and the usher pulled him out to the aisle, stood him up and asked what he was doing. "I was in the balcony listening to the concert and got excited and fell over the railing," was the reply.

Pianist: "They tell me you love fine music, is that right?"

Patron: "You got that right. But don't let it bother you — just keep on playing."

The Conductor

This Backward Man, this View Obstructor
Is known to us as the CONDUCTOR.
He beats the time with grace and vim
And sometimes they keep up with him.
But though they're eloquent and snappy
Conductors always seem unhappy.
Their strange grimaces on the podium
Suggest bicarbonate of sodium.
May be, perhaps, the proper diet
To keep their inner fires quiet.
They have to think up countless capers
To keep them in the daily papers
Which help them in financial strictures
Or fit them for the motion pictures.
Conductors worry all the while
That's why they bow, but never smile.

Laurence McKinney, *People of Note*
(Out of print for nearly 30 years, will be
re-released in 1999. If you can't find
a copy, try Amazon.com on the internet)

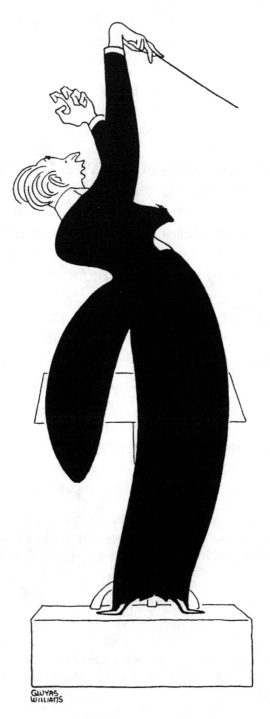

Mabel: "Did you hear about the planeload of symphonic conductors on an airplane that crashed?"

Hazel: "No! Tell me about it."

Mabel: "The good news is that it crashed. The bad news is that there were four empty seats!"

Applause is a receipt, not necessarily a note of demand.

Praise of a composer: What he receives after he is dead.

"Oh, George, isn't this music heavenly?"

"Hmmm, Honey, I think you've got your directions mixed."

Jay: "How did you like the symphony last night? It was my first experience as conductor!"

Fay: "Please, not while I'm eating!"

Last year, I gave several lectures on "Intelligence and Musicality in Animals." Today, I shall speak to you about the "Intelligence and Musicality in Critics." The subjects are very similar.

Erik Satie

Wife: "How did you enjoy the symphony last night?"

Hubby: "I felt real good after it — like a new man when I woke up!"

Larry: "What do you get when you toss a symphony conductor off a 20-story building?"
Harry: "Lots of applause!"

One time, Leonard Bernstein, Herbert Van Karajian, and Theobald Bohm were having coffee at the café while discussing who was the greatest ever of conductors.

"Gentleman," said Von Karajian, "I am absolutely the greatest conductor this world has ever seen."

"That's just not so," said Lenny. "Just last evening, the Lord spoke to me and said: 'Lenny, your direction of Beethoven's *Fifth Symphony* was the best since the beginning of time'."

Just then, Theobald yelled: "LIAR! I never once said anything like that!"

The amateur conductor had his entire string ensemble at his home for practice when there came a knock on the door. The conductor halted the group, went to the door, and found a policeman standing there. "Sir," said the policeman, "I need to come in your home and look around."

"But why?" asked the conductor/homeowner.

"Well, we had a report from your neighbor to come here because someone was murdering Wagner."

Composers should write tunes that chauffeurs and errand boys can whistle.

Sir Thomas Beecham

Music is the refuge of souls ulcerated by happiness.

E. M. Cioran

Professor: "How was your recital last night at Carnegie Hall?"

Student: "Great! After it, I went down and shook hands with the audience."

Professor: "How nice. "I'm pleased to know you shook hands with him!"

"Ninety-seven dollars? Good heavens, who tuned it? Leonard Bernstein?"

Jim: "Why did J. S. Bach have twenty children?"
Tim: "Because his organ had no stops!"

197

At the symphony concert, his date turned to him and asked, "Dear, what's that book the conductor keeps looking at?"

"That, dear Anna," her date responded, "is the score of the symphony."

"Really! Well, could you tip me off as to who's ahead?"

Edith studied classical music but Al never got beyond, "Yessir! That's My Baby!" They were immersed in a discussion about music and, eventually, the conversation got around to the Norwegian composer Edvard Grieg.

"I just love his music," Edith said. "He is simply incomparable in the world of symphonic music."

"Maybeso," responded Al, "but the jerk couldn't even spell his first name right!"

At a concert with amateur musicians, it is difficult to know whether the musicians are playing a melody or tuning their instruments.

If you have a sore throat and a bad cough, you should go to the doctor. But if you won't, you'll go to the symphony concert.

"George, why is it that you prefer Wagner's music to all others?"

"Well, Pete, I can always hear it above the surrounding conversations."

What is the implement of preference when symphony musicians wish to sip a drink?
Orchestraws!

"How do you tell the difference between a bull and a symphony orchestra?"
"The bull has the horns in front and the ass in back."

When a piece gets difficult, make faces.

Arthur Schnabel to Vladimir Horowitz

"What are you going to play next, Maestro?"
"I like it when you call me Maestro — it gives me that international aroma."
"Garlic will do the same."

The symphony was delighted to learn that a deceased admirer of the theirs had left them his entire estate except for one heir who sued for his share. The judge asked the directors of the symphony what percentage of the estate they wanted to leave for the heir, and they replied: "He gets one-tenth of the estate and we'll keep the other nine."

The judge reversed this, saying: "So, you take the tenth part and leave the balance for the heir because the will states: 'He shall have whatever pleases you.'"

David Raskin, a most dedicated musician, a man who has written the musical scores for dozens of films, once mentioned to a friend that he was going to write the musical score for Alfred Hitchcock's latest film, *Lifeboat.*

"I don't think you'll get to do it," his friend replied. "I heard he's not going to have any music in the show."

"You gotta be wrong," was the response.

"Just think about it. There they are, way out in the ocean in a lifeboat and no musicians within a thousand miles. Nobody expects to hear music in that scene!"

"Well, to be perfectly logical," David Raskin replied, "if you'll consider just where the cameras come from in the middle of the ocean, you'll know exactly where my music will come from."

The conductor danced three times with the pretty orchestra harpist. The harpist was flattered and told him so.

"I didn't intend it as a compliment," he told her.

"Then why did you dance so much with me alone?" she asked.

"I hate dancing," he replied. "I only dance because I like to sweat."

A British symphony orchestra arrived in America for its first time in the country. The first night, the leader had just gone to bed when an owl hooted loudly outside the hotel window.

"Don't worry and let it upset you," said his American assistant. "It's only an owl."

"I know that," responded the Englishman, "but 'oo's' owling?"

A doctor and a conductor were arguing about whose profession was the oldest.

"Ours has to be," said the musician, "because the trumpets announced Joshua's battle of Jericho."

"That may be true," said the physician, "but please remember that when Adam had to lose a rib to make Eve, a doctor had to do the delivery and administer care after removal."

Classical music is the kind we keep thinking will turn into a tune.

Kin Hubbard
Abe Martin's Sayings, 1915

We cannot expect you to be with us all the time, but perhaps you could be good enough to keep in touch now and again.

Sir Thomas Beecham
(request to his violin section)

During the performance of a work by Carl Ruggles (1876-1971), the composer leaped to his feet to confront a disrupter. "Stop being such a damned fool!" he yelled. "Stand up and use your ears like a man!"

Mrs. Eaton loved symphony music but hubby Elmer hated it. Still, on this one night, the Mrs. managed to drag Elmer to the concert. But Elmer managed to delay things before they left, saying he had to do this and then that. He was so successful with his delaying tactics that they arrived at the concert hall at 9:45 P.M.! They took seats and Mrs. Eaton picked up the program, looked at it, then said, "Oh my! We're now in the last movement of Beethoven's Ninth Symphony."

"That's great!" responded Elmer, "I'm sure tickled pink that we missed the first eight!"

A patron at a symphony concert asked the orchestra conductor: "Sir, does your orchestra ever play requests?"

Conductor: "We do. What would you like to request of us?"

"Ask them to play poker."

The young guy kept talking during a symphony concert, disturbing the man seated behind him. "What a spoilsport, a nuisance." The man exclaimed.

"Are you referring to me?" the young guy in front exclaimed, turning around to face the man behind.

"Oh, no," replied the man. "I mean the musicians up on stage. They make so damned much noise that I can't hear your conversation!"

A beggar who had just been given a coin by the symphony conductor said: "Thank you so much. I hope you and your family will be in heaven tonight."

"I know you mean well," responded the conductor, "but please don't hurry us in this matter!"

There was a small-town orchestra that was to have an important concert to be held in six months. At each rehearsal, there was always one musician missing! But the violinist was always there — never missed!

On the day of the concert, at the final rehearsal preceding the performance, the conductor said: "Tonight is our big night. It's been tough on me having so many of you miss rehearsals. Only one of you, our violinist, Pete Elrod, never missed a rehearsal."

"That's the very least I could do," responded Pete, "seeing I'm not gonna show up at tonight's concert!"

The sound audiences make during a concert sounds more like the plural of ZZZZZ.

It is quite untrue that the English people don't appreciate symphony music. They may not understand it but they absolutely love the noise it makes.

Sir Thomas Beecham

"What have you got when a trainload of conductors ends up in a pit of concrete up to their necks?"

"Not enough concrete."

You should never trust anyone who listens to Mahler before they're forty.

Clive James

Show me a noted and famous conductor's liquor cabinet and I'll show you Beethoven's Fifth.

In music, one must think with the heart and feel with the brain.

George Szell

The leading violinist of the symphony had just had her first baby and when she returned to the orchestra, she was asked what name she had chosen. "Opium is her name," she answered.

"But why Opium?" she was asked.

"Because opium comes from wild poppies and her poppy is certainly wild!"

A music lecture was taking place in New Hampshire. With constant repetition, the lecturer kept saying that art could not improve upon nature.

Finally, in exasperation, one listener said, "Oh no? How would you look without your wig!"

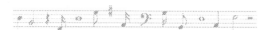

From the start of his career, composer George Gershwin had faith in himself. He used to praise his mother by explaining, "She is so modest about *me*."

During a frightful electrical storm, the conductor was the only one of the entire symphony and its travel crew willing to go out in the awful storm and get the bus. Why was the leader of the symphony so fearless?

Simply because he knew he was a poor conductor!

Some conductors take pains with their music while others give them.

A vacationing symphony composer was attending a concert, and the orchestra was playing *The Magic Flute*. His neighbor turned and asked in a whisper, "Who composed this number?"

"Mozart," replied the conductor.

"Mozart? Well, I guess I never heard of him. Is he still composing?"

"No, Madam. He is decomposing."

Tonic: A kind of medicine frequently taken by musicians before performing and always after the performance.

Conductor: A person who makes you face the music.

How To Understand Music

With people having the Very Best Music interpreted for them every Sunday afternoon over the radio by the Very Best Experts, it will soon be so that we can't hear "Turkey in the Straw" without reading a meaning into it. With so much attention being paid to *leitmotifs* and the inner significance of what the bassoons are saying, it would not be surprising if, after a while, we forgot to beat time. And if you don't beat time, where is your music?

I would like to take up this afternoon an analysis of Bach's "Carry Me Back to Old Virginny" symphonic Tschaikovski in C minor, one of the loveliest, and, at the same time, one of the most difficult exercises for three-and-a-half fingers ever written. I may have to stop and lie down every few minutes during my interpretation, it is so exciting. You may do as you like while I am lying down.

In the first place, I must tell you that the modern works of Sch(nberg, although considerably incomprehensible to the normal ear (that is, an ear which adheres rather closely to the head and *looks* like an ear) are, in reality, quite significant to those who are on the inside. This includes Schonberg himself, his father, and a young man in whom he confides while dazed. What you think are random noises made by the musicians falling over forward on their instruments, are, when you understand them, really steps in a great, moving story — the Story of the Traveling Salesman who Came to the Farmhouse. If you have heard it, try to stop me.

We first have the introduction by the woodwinds, in which you will detect the approach of summer, the bassoons indicating the bursting buds (summer and spring came together this year, almost before we were aware of it) and the brasses carrying the idea of winter disappearing, defeated and ashamed, around the corner. Summer approaches (in those sections where you hear the "tum-tiddy-ump-ump-tum-tiddy-ump-ump." Remember?) and then, taking one look around, decides that the whole thing is hardly worth while, and goes back into its hole — a new and not entirely satisfactory union of the groundhog tradition with that of the equinox. This, however, ends the first movement, much to the relief of every one.

You will have noticed that during this depicting of the solstice, the wind section has been forming dark colors right and left, all typical of Tschaikovski in his more woodwind moods. These dark colors, such as purple, green, and sometimes W and Y, are very lovely once they are recognized. The difficulty comes in recognizing them, especially with beards on. The call of the clarinet, occurring at intervals during this first movement, is clearly the voice of summer, saying, "Co-boss! Co-boss! Co-boss!" To which the tympani reply, "Rumble-rumble-rumble!" And a very good reply it is, too.

The second movement begins with Strephon (the eternal shepherd, and something of a bore) dancing up to the hut in which Phyllis is weaving honey, and, by means of a series of descending six-four chords, as in Debussy's "Reflets dans l'eau" (which, you will remember, also makes no sense), indicating that he is ready for a romp. Here we hear the dripping coolness of the mountain stream and the jump-jump-jump of the mountain goat, neither of which figures in the story. He is very eager (tar-ra-ty-tar-ra-ty-tar-ra-ty) and says that there is no sense in her being difficult about the thing, for he has everything arranged. At this the oboes go crazy.

I like to think that the two most obvious modulations, the dominant and the subdominant respectively, convey the idea that, whatever it is that Strephon is saying to Phyllis, nobody cares. This would make the whole thing much clearer. The transition from the dominant to the subdominant (or, if you prefer, you may stop over at Chicago for a day and see the bullfights) gives a feeling of adventure, a sort of Old Man River note, which, to me, is most exciting. But then, I am easily excited.

We now come to the third movement, if there is anybody left in the hall. The third movement is the most difficult to understand, as it involves a complete reversal of musical form in which the woodwinds play the brasses, the brasses play the tympani, and the tympani play "drop-the-handkerchief." This makes for confusion, as you may very well guess. But, as confusion is the idea, the composer is sitting pretty and the orchestra has had its exercise. The chief difficulty in this movement lies in keep the A-strings so tuned that they sound like B-flat strings. To this end, small boys are employed to keep turning the pegs down and the room is kept as damp as possible.

It is here that Arthur, a character who has, up until now, taken no part in the composition, appears and, just as at the rise of the sixth in Chopin's "Nocturne in E Flat" one feels a certain elation, tells Strephon that he has already made plans for Phyllis for that evening and will he please get the hell out of here. We feel, in the descent of the fourth, that Strephon is saying "So what?" to any movement in which occurs a rise from the key-note to the major third. Get right on that, please, and a similar rise to the minor third, or, if you happen to own a bit of U.S. Steel, a rise to 56, suggests a possibility of future comfort. All this, however, is beside the point. (Dorothy Angus, of 1455 Granger Drive, Salt Lake City, has just telephoned in to ask "What point?" Any point, Dorothy, any point. When you are older, you will understand.)

This brings us to the fourth movement, which we will omit, owing to one of the oboes having clamped his teeth down so hard on his mouthpiece as to make further playing a mockery.

I am very sorry about this, as the fourth movement has in it, one of my favorite passages — that where Strephon unbuttons his coat.

From now on, it is anybody's game. The A minor prelude, with its persistent chromatic descent, conflicts with the *andante sostenuto*, where the strings take the melody in bars 7 and 8, and the undeniably witty theme is carried on to its logical conclusion in bars 28 and 30, where the pay-off comes then the man tells his wife that he was in the pantry all the time. I nearly die at this every time that I hear it. Unfortunately, I don't hear it often enough, or long enough at a time.

This, in a way, brings to a close our little analysis of whatever it was we were analyzing. If I have made music a little more difficult for you to like, if I have brought confusion into your ear and complication into your taste, I shall be happy in the thought. The next time you hear a symphony, I trust that you will stop all this silly sitting back and taking it for what it is worth to your ear-drums and to your emotions, and will put on your thinking caps and try to figure out just what the composer meant when he wrote it. Then perhaps you will write and tell the composer.

NO POEMS SOAR (Around the World
Backwards, Forewords and Sideways)
Robert Benchley. 1932
New York: Harper & Bros., Publishers

CHAPTER EIGHT

Winds

A boy who played tunes on a comb,
Had become such a nuisance at home.
His mom spanked him and then asked:
"Will you do it again?"
And he dutifully answered, Nomb."

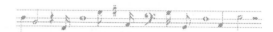

The two clarinetists were neighbors and each one had a dog he loved. The one man drove his car over the other's dog, killing it. The bereaved was furious, shouting obscenities right and left at his neighbor-clarinetist.

"I really didn't realize how much of a relative of yours he was," was the reply of the guilty neighbor, to the tirade.

Elmer: "What does an oboe player call a diminished fifth?"

Ralph: "An almost finished bottle of bourbon."

Dick: "I just killed a saxophone player."

Rick: "That can't be a capital offense. What do you think you'll get?"

Dick: "Some sleep."

English Horn

The ENGLISH HORN I must reveal
Has no connection with John Peal;
In fact Old John would find it meaner
To play on than a vacuum cleaner.
It's tone would make his horses skittish
For it is neither horn — nor British.
Some call it to increase this tangle —
The Cor Anglais — or horn with angle —
Concerning which I'm glad to state
The English Horn is long and straight.
Its misery and constant dwelling
On tragedy has caused a swelling
Just where the doleful note emerges;
Imbued with melancholy surges
This makes an English Horn cadenza
Sound fearfully like influenza.

Laurence McKinney, *People of Note*
(Out of print for nearly 30 years, will be
re-released in 1999. If you can't locate
a copy, try Amazon.com on the internet)

GLUYAS
WILLIAMS

Joe: "You know, you remind me of a clarinet."
Moe: "But a clarinet is a wood instrument!"
Joe: "Y'know! You just got the idea!"

An English horn is a bazooka with a college degree.

There was a young lady of Rio,
Who essayed to take part in a trio;
But her skill was so scanty
She played it andante
Instead of allegro con brio!

Saxophone: It's an ill wind that blows most saxophones.
Some call it not a musical instrument but a weapon. He who
plays one need not have a sense of harmony but plenty of
hush money.

Molly: "What's the difference between a dog and an
oboe player?"
Polly: "The dog knows when to stop scratching."

The audience was still applauding the first number rendered by the Wappingdale Falls Marching and Chowder
Club Band when the trombonist leaned over and asked the
flute player, "What number do we do next?" "The
Washington Post March," answered the flute player. "Holy
cow," gasped the trombonist. "That's what I just finished
playing!"

213

The saxophone is the embodied spirit of beer.
Arnold Bennettn
(1867-1931)

The chief objection to playing a wind instrument is that it prolongs the life of the player.
George Bernard Shawn
(1856-1950)

Saturday Evening Post Album: 1975-1985
Reprinted with permission of The
Saturday Evening Post Society

Q: "Why does a chicken cross the road?"
A: "It wants to get away from the oboe recital."

A fellow once bought his wife a piano for Christmas, but by Mother's Day, he had persuaded her to switch to the oboe. "But why?" asked a friend.

214

"Because," the fellow replied, "when she's playing the oboe, she can't sing."

Trill: About the same sound as a frightful epileptic seizure.

A tooter who tooted a flute,
Tried to teach two young tooters to toot;
Said the two to the tooter,
"Is it harder to toot or
To tutor two tooters to toot?

Carolyn Wells
Book of American Limericks
London: G. P. Putnam & Sons, 1925

Teacher: "Please give us your definition of a gentlemen."
Student: "A person who knows how to play the bassoon but doesn't."

Manager: "How do you get someone to stop trampling on a saxophone?"
Conductor: "Why would you want to stop them?"

Joe: "What's the distinction between a power mower and a tenor sax?"
Floe: "Your neighbor gets really mad if you don't return the power mower."

The lad finished his flute solo and returned to his seat. The boy sitting behind him tapped his shoulder and said, "Buddy, that was something! You ought to be on TV!"

"Gee, thanks," replied the young flutist. "But do you really think I'm that good?"

"No, but a least I could push the 'off' button!"

All the musicians of the Everest Symphony Orchestra were first-rate musicians — except for one! And that one, well, every time he opened his mouth, he put his oboe into it!

Two clarinet players were walking down the street when one said: "Tell me, Joe, who was that flute I saw you walking with last night?"

"That wasn't a flute, man, that was my fife."

Conductor: "What's the difference between the sound of an oboe and a cat in heat?"

Vet: "There is none — if the cat is healthy!"

Two fellows walk together down the street, one is a bassoonist and the other is an oboist who doesn't have any money either.

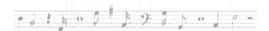

Musician: "How can you get four oboe players to play in tune?"

Conductor: "Shoot three of 'em."

The Bass Flute

The Bassethorn

The orchestra director raised his hand, and tapped his stand to stop the rehearsal. "Why did you stop playing when we got to the chorus?" he asked the clarinetist.

"I did just what the music demanded," the lad replied. "It said — REFRAIN — and I did."

Oboe: A cockney tramp.

Lines to a Saxophone

You blear, barbaric beast,
  I've often heard you moan,
And passionately pant and sigh,
  And gargle, grunt and groan,
I've heard you stammer, heard you sneeze,
  I've listened to your neigh,
I've heard you cough and snort and wheeze,
  But I've never heard you *play*.

I've heard you crow all night,
  And gurgle, spit and squeak,
I've heard you nicker, heard you bark
  And squall and scream and shriek;
I've heard you hiccough, heard you howl,
  And listened to your bay,
I've heard you grumble, heard you growl,
  But I've never heard you *play*.

I've heard your guttural gamut,
  With the accent on the gutter,
I've speared your suspirations
  And I hate the noise you utter;
I have heard you bleat and blather,
  I have heard you bawl and bray,
Heard you worked up to a lather —
  But I've *never* heard you *play*.

Source Unknown

218

A musician was taking a walk one day, when suddenly an elf appeared and offered him one free wish. The musician takes his pocket atlas and showed the elf certain countries. "Notice that here there is hunger and over there people are suffering disease and in the next place, you see torture being used. Now! I wish all folks to be healthy and free from tyranny. Can you help me with that?"

The elf shook his head and said, "You've given me a tough chore, Pardner. Can't you give me something a teeny bit easier to do for you?"

"Yeah, I can," the musician replied. "Y'see, I play clarinet and I have a hard time with the intonation in the top register. Can you help me?"

Elf: "Let me take another look at that pocket atlas."

A Scotsman lay dying in a New York hospital and his doctor told the nurse to give him anything he wanted. So the guy said that before he died, he'd love to hear a piece or two of bagpipe music. So the nurse obliged him and a piper came and played for the dying Scotsman. And do you know, that Scotsman recovered 100%, but all the other patients on the floor died.

219

Q: Why are bass fiddle jokes so short?
A: So clarinetists can understand them.

Angels' Instrument: Thank goodness that heaven selected its musical instruments before the uke and the sax were
invented.

Andrew Carnegie was fond of the bagpipe. When he
dined at his home at Skibo Castle, he usually had his pet
piper play for him. The musician was always in attendance
when the great philanthropist had guests.

One time, a company of men sat down to the table and
the piper pranced up and down the room as he played.

The whole thing was new to a literary man, who politely
asked the guest on his right, "Why does he walk up and
down when he plays this thing? Does it add volume or does
it make a cadence?"

"Nither," said the other. "I think it's to prevent the listen-
ers from getting his range with a knife or plate or with a
water bottle."

Larry: "If you were asked to make a bass saxophone
sound like a chainsaw, how would you do it?"
Terry: "Add *vibrato*."

Flute

First of the woodwinds we salute
The clever rogue who plays the FLUTE.
He points his pipe the other way
Fixes his lips and starts to play.

To sound those notes, so chaste, so pure —
He blows across the embouchure
Which gives him, pardon the digression,
A strangely, squirrel-like expression.
These queer high-handed players know
Another trick — the PICCOLO —
Just half as long and twice as shrill
It paralyses ears at will
(Our artist, I deplore the fact,
Has caught him in the very act.)
The flautist's task is the pursuit
Of toot and nothing but the toot.

> Laurence McKinney, *People of Note*
> (Out of print for nearly 30 years, will be
> re-printed in 1999. If you can't locate
> a copy, try Amazon.com on the internet)

BILL
HARRISON

"Look, why don't you put that thing away and neck for a while?"

> Reprinted with permission of The
> Saturday Evening Post Society

Old John Petefish, the town critic, was informed that Edgar Eldridge, the richest man in the village, owned a violin 200 years old.

"Beats the hell out of me," John said, "why that old geezer doesn't throw that old fiddle away and buy him a new one. Lord knows he can afford it!"

After the concert, the oboe player went up to a lovely girl from the audience. But he got nowhere. She told him to keep his dissonance!

"Music in every room"

A talented young lady named Dager
Who as the result of a wager,
Consented to fart the complete clarinet part,
Of the Mozart Quartet in G Major.

An amateur flautist stopped in at a music store to consider a fine recording system. The salesman worked hard to sell him and finally said, "I see you have your instrument with you. Why not record something and see how you like what the machine does?"

So the flautist took out his instrument and played into the recorder and the salesman listened. When finished, the salesman said. "Now would you like to buy the recorder?"

"No," said the flautist, "but I'll sell my flute!"

He's so dumb, he put his saxophone in the refrigerator to get some cool music.

Joe: "Man, I feel fit as a fiddle."
Moe: "That's funny — you look more like a saxophone."

During the playing of *Stars and Stripes Forever*, the piccolo player stepped to the front and began his stirring piccolo solo. When he had finished, a voice in the audience roared, "That piccolo player is a sonovabitch!"

The conductor turned and yelled to the audience, "Who called that piccolo player an s.o.b.?"

Voice from the audience replied: "Who called that s.o.b. a piccolo player?"

"Elmer," said the teacher, "if you don't show more interest in learning to play the oboe, I'll tell your folks that you are really talented!"

"How come you put your saxophone up for sale, Lester?"

"I came home one day and saw my next-door-neighbor out in his backyard sharpening his machete!"

Teacher: "How would you describe "perfect pitch"?"

Drummer: "Well, the best way to arrive at it is when you lob an oboist into a garbage can without hitting the rim."

"Maybe your pet would stop screaming if you didn't squeeze him so hard."

An amateur musician was making gruesome sounds on his saxophone at midnight when the outraged landlord burst into his apartment and roared, "Do you know there's two little old ladies sick upstairs?"

"I don't think I do," replied the amateur. "Would you hum the first few bars of it?"

Oboe

Hard to pronounce and play, the OBOE —
(With cultured folk it rhymes with "doughboy"
Though many an intellectual hobo
Insists that we should call it oboe)
However, be that as it may,
Whene'er the oboe sounds its A
All of the others start their tuning
And there is fiddling and bassooning.
Its plaintive note presaging gloom
Brings anguish to the concert room
Even the player holds his breath
And scares the audience to death
For fear he may get off the key,
Which happens not infrequently.
This makes the saying understood:
"It's an ill wood wind no one blows good."

Laurence McKinney, *People of Note*

Band leader: "Why do clarinetists prefer to march while they play?"

Manager: "Because it is harder to hit a moving target!"

TOM HENDERSON

"Compliments of the folks at table ten."

Nostrilala: An unusual sound of musical tone achieved while blowing the nose.

CHAPTER NINE

Brass

My friend was an unsuccessful entrepreneur. Example: He bought an office building and put music in all the elevators — a live band in each. Now do you understand his business difficulties?

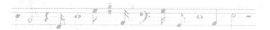

Q: "Why do saxophone players have brains the size of a bean?"

A: "Because excessive intake of whiskey has swollen them."

Taxpayers anthem: "My Country, It Is Not Free."

"And you'll be happy to know my new boyfriend doesn't play a guitar."

"Did you ever hear anything so beautiful?" said the daughter to her father as her new rap tape played.

"Nope, never have," replied her father. "Closest thing to it that I've ever heard was a collision of one truck loaded with empty steel barrels and the other truck loaded with hogs."

Conductor: "What do fellow symphonists call a tuba player with half a brain?"

Manager: "Musically gifted."

Two cornetists hated each other, but one day one of them had to go to the other's home and did so. But his hated rival wasn't home so he scrawled the name "Bastard" on the door and left.

Later that day, the man returned home and saw the name on the door and left immediately to settle things with his enemy, but he wasn't home.

Later that night the man on whose door the epithet was written was asked by his wife why he had tried to go to the home of his enemy.

"Well, he wrote his name on my door, so I thought I'd find out what he wanted," was the reply.

Jazz will endure just as long as people hear it through their feet instead of their brain.

John Phillip Sousa
(1854-1932)

Let a short Act of Parliament be passed, placing all street musicians outside the protection of the law, so that

any citizen may assail them with stones, sticks, knives, pis-
tols, or bombs without incurring any penalties

George Bernard Shaw

"This should be interesting."

Reprinted with permission of The
Saturday Evening Post Society

A crooner's admirer ran up to him after the concert and
said, "You sang 'Lilacs in the Rain' just beautifully, so beautifully that I could even smell the lilacs."

"But what about my voice, the melody as I sang it?" the
singer asked. "Did you like it, too?"

"Oh yes, I could smell your voice, too."

The conductor was having a rehearsal and was especially concerned with the mistakes of the tuba player. Finally, he
stopped the orchestra and demanded of the tuba player:
"What's wrong with you man? You're doing a terrible job!"

"I know it, Maestro," moaned the tuba player. "I blow into this horn so nice and sweet but it comes out just awful."

Two publishers of music were discussing a new jazz piece:

"I've never heard such corny lyrics, such simpering senti-mentality, such repetitious, uninspired melody. Man, we've got a hit on our hands!"

Brad Anderson

The band music of a marriage procession always reminds me of the music of soldiers marching to battle.

Heinrich Heine
(1797-1856)

You ask: "What time is it when your clothes get full of holes and they wear out?"
Answer: "Beats me."
Reply: "Ragtime!"

"Are you sure you're able to lead a heavy metal band?"
"I sure am. I've been shell-shocked in the army, had a nervous breakdown and raised twelve kids!"

Who were these guys?
Four jolly guys sat down to play,
They played all night till break of day;
They played for bucks and not for fun,
With a different score for every one,
Yet when they came to square accounts,
Each one had made very fair amounts!
Can you this paradox explain?
Cause if no one lost, how could all gain?
Answer: They were all musicians in a jazz band!

Author Unknown

Jazz is music invented by devils for the torture of imbeciles.

Henry Van Dyke (1852-1933)

You have to blame Thomas Alva Edison for rock 'n roll. He invented electricity.

"Why don't you just try reading yourself to sleep?"

Teacher: "How does a musician clean a dirty tuba?"
Student: "With a tuba toothpaste, of course!"

The teacher was eating in the school cafeteria and nudged her dinner companion: "I want you to notice that girl over there. Do you see just how gracefully she eats her corn on the cob?"

"She ought to," responded the other, "she plays the piccolo in the school band!"

If you are not afraid to face the music, you may get to lead the band some day.

Edwin H. Stuart

"Why can't he just howl at the moon like other dogs?"

"Once I did play the violin in the symphony but I had to quit it."

"Really? Why was that?"

"Well, I was seated in front of the trombonist and got nothing but bumps on the back of my head."

"What's a skeleton's favorite musical instrument?"
"The tromBONE!"

Harry: "Why are trumpet players buried eight feet deep?"
Larry: "Because way down deep, they are (honestly) real nice folks!"

Usher: "How do you make a trumpet player angry?"
Conductor: "Call him an oboist!"

Two ladies were discussing their sons and one of them
said to the other: "My son has asked a lovely girl, daughter
of our banker, to marry him. He told her he was near the top
of TV brass."
"Just wait till she finds out he plays trombone in the
orchestra!"

Q: "What's the difference between a trumpet and a chain
saw?"
A: "Who knows?"

"Hey, I found a dime!"

Reporter: "How would you define musical rap?"
Conductor: "I'd call it audible graffiti."

Jazz is a kind and healing form of music. To understand just why that is so, think of all the people who would go to jail for lewd conduct if they danced without music!

The father ran into the school's band director on the street. He asked: "How's my boy doing. Is he playing well for you?"

"Oh, very well. He's doing fine."

"Glad to hear that," said Dad. "I was beginning to feel that I was merely getting used to it."

It was back in rock-and-roll days with such things as discotheque. Once, while the "dance" music paused, the girl turned to her partner and thanked him for dancing with her.

"Why do you think I was dancing?" the lad exclaimed. "I was just looking for the toilet!"

I always have trouble singing *The Star Spangled Banner*. The only time I can hit those high notes is when I back into a doorknob!

Joe came to the office looking as though he hadn't slept well. A fellow worker asked if he were ill.

"No, I'm fine," Joe said. " It's just that the people upstairs kept tromping and tromping on the floor above my apartment."

"I guess that kept you from sleeping?"

"Nope. I just kept on practicing my tuba."

Teenager in a music store: "I'm looking for a song that goes, 'Umpity-Bumpity-Zoom-Kerbang-Zoom."

Clerk: "What are the words to that song?"

Teenager: "*Those* are the words, stupid!"

This advertisement appeared in a small town Iowa newspaper: "Wanted: to trade saxophone with case for fresh cow."

"Tell me, Stan, why are you so popular in your neighborhood?"

"Well, y'see, I play the trumpet and I told my neighbors I only play it when I'm lonely."

"Does my practicing the trumpet bother you?" the man asked of his next-door-neighbor.

"It did at first," the neighbor replied, "but after I heard all the neighbors discussing it and you, I decided that I didn't give a damn what happened to you!"

The new music teacher at a boys' school had organized a new band, and the principal decided the band should make its debut before their teacher felt it was ready. So, on performance day, he tapped the music stand and hissed at his young musicians, "If you don't feel sure of your part, just pretend to play."

Then he brought his baton down with a magnificent flourish — and the entire band gave forth with an overwhelming silence.

"Well, military school was your idea!"

Cartoon Festival 1958
Reprinted with permission of The
Saturday Evening Post Society

Carlyle's definition of classical music is as applicable to jazz as to serious music: a creation of the devil to delight idiots.

"I said 'tea and crumpets!'"

At the head of the list of modern composers is the tranquilizer.

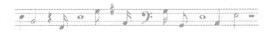

Singer: "What is the difference between a dead snake and a dead trombonist on a dirt road?"
Drummer: "There are skid marks in front of the snake."

The new arrival had scarcely entered heaven when St. Peter stepped up and presented him with a beautiful golden trumpet. "But, I can't play this instrument," protested the newcomer. "I never practiced while I was on earth."

"I know you didn't," chuckled St. Peter. "That's why you're here."

Fireman: "How do you get a euphonium player out of a tree?"

Conductor: "Cut the rope!"

TUTLOW MUSICAL INSTRUMENTS

PRES.

Mittlebeeler   Saturday Evening Post

"Probably going to declare a dividend."

Reprinted with permission of The Saturday Evening Post Society

Teacher: "How would you describe the difference between a sousaphonist and the rear end of a horse?"

Student: "Sorry! I can't help you on that one!"

"How come you advertised your cornet for sale?" asked a friend of his musician neighbor. "I thought you loved to play that instrument."

"I sure did enjoy it." His friend replied. "But when I saw my neighbor in K-mart buying a shotgun, I figured I really ought to get rid of my cornet!"

The town's brass band had just finished a loud but not very coordinated selection. The musicians had just sunk down to their seats after bowing to the applause when the trombonist asked: "What are we playing next?"

The band director replied: "The Stars and Stripes Forever."

"Oh my gosh!" exploded the trombonist, "I just got through playing that!"

Violinist: "What do four trombonists sound like when they play from the bottom of the lake?"

Drummer: "Sounds like a great idea!"

"Way back when" they told the story of the famed French horn player who let his wig fall down the horn of his instrument. He spent the rest of the evening "blowing his top"!

A musician went to a real estate agent and said: "I want to buy a house but it has to be at least a mile from any other house."

"But tell me why does it have to be so far removed?" the real estate agent asked.

"Because I intend to practice my French horn," was the reply.

Student to neighbor: "I'm going away to study trumpet."
Neighbor: "Good! How far away?"

Q: "Why did the students complain about their band director?"
A: "Because he was entirely too hot-tempoed!"

Little Ernest was only 5-years-old when he went to the park with his grandfather to hear the municipal band play. After they'd listened for a while and the band had come to an in-between-pieces halt, Ernest turned to his grandfather and asked: "That's your kind of noise, isn't it, Grandpa?"

My trombone looks much better than I do in my derby.

Ernie: "Why is playing the tuba like wetting your pants?"
Bernie: "Because both give you that warm, glowing feeling!"

Trombone: An instrument useful for getting even with the musician in front of the player, when aimed at his head.

Brass bands are all very well in their place — outdoors and several miles away!

Sir Thomas Beechamn
(1879-1961)

©1990 Post Dispatch Features, all rights reserved

"His playing certainly sounds screechy...which reminds me — where's the cat today?"

You don't have to be tone deaf to write a jazzy song, but it sure helps.

Many a song would be on the Hit Parade except for two things — the words and the music.

Sweet popular music is clap-trap in the main and in the main is where it belongs.

Peter DeVries

So far, the greatest martial music ever written is the wedding march.

Last night, the band played Beethoven. Beethoven lost.

Anonymous

Manager: "What is the difference between a bag of manure and a band director?"
Janitor: "The bag."

Trombonist: A man who succeeds by blowing his own horn and letting things slide.

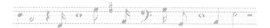

Define "bar line".
A group of trumpet players at a popular hootch gallery.

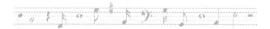

He composes music in bed. He calls it "sheet music".

There was a sign in a Chicago newspaper that read: "For Sale. A large group of rock-and-roll and be-bop music. Call us, but if a boy answers, hang up and call later."

One day Dad asked his son what he wanted to be when he grew up. The boy replied, "Pop, I'm nuts about jazz. I want to be a jazz musician."

"Drop that idea, Son," Dad replied. "You can't have it both ways."

"Kitchy-Koo!"

The teenage daughter of the house had just finished playing a contemporary jazz disc. She turned to her father to ask: "Did you ever hear anything as beautiful as that, Daddy?"

"Nope. Sure haven't. The closest thing to it I've ever heard was when a truck loaded with empty milk cans collided with another truck loaded with pigs and, well, the resulting sounds were very similar!"

The only typical American music is that made by the canary, the saxophone and the cash register.

Someone once explained the excellent acoustics of a concert hall by saying, "It's the building. The acoustics here would make a fart sound like a sevenfold amen."

"I don't know what to do," little Jimmy complained to his mother. "You tell me to practice and the neighbors tell me to stop."

"He's a music arranger."
"I wish he'd do something for my brother."
"What would you like him to arrange for your brother?"
"To get his saxophone out of the pawnshop."

I only know two tunes. One of them is "Yankee Doodle Dandy" and the other isn't.

Ulysses S. Grant

Classical music is music without words, while modern music is music without music.

"All right, who put bubblegum in my tuba?"

A critic is a necessary evil, and criticism is an evil necessity.

Carolyn Wells
(1869-1942)

An English horn teacher: A Tudor tooter tutor.

Laughter from the Hip

Kay Starr: My greatest musical education was during my four years with the Joe Venuti band.

In one town we visited, the manager of the place we were supposed to play came up to Joe and said, "There's a War Bond drive on, and they want you to play a broadcast at the local radio station."

Well, we had just finished setting up the bandstand, and it would all have to be taken down again and hauled to the station so Joe was just a little hacked about it. But we took it down and showed up at the station.

During the War Bond days, they were forever putting people in charge of shows of this kind who really didn't know what it was all about. The least musically knowledgeable people were put in charge of things that needed the most imagination. We got one of those colonels or majors or something who was very smitten with his own importance. And there's nothing that annoys Joe more than somebody that's in an important position and doesn't deserve to be there.

This fellow is telling Joe things like, "You're not playing enough fast songs and too many slow songs." All of a sudden, he was a music director.

All we wanted to do was do the show and get out of there and have a few minutes' rest before we did our regular show, because we'd been driving all night and we were all dead tired. So Joe says, "Okay, feller, just tell me what you want."

The major goes into the control room. Now he wants to check the sound level on everything. Then he starts this routine with, "No, the saxophones are too close," and "Joe, back a little further," until finally Joe couldn't take it any more. And he says, "We're going to have to take a rest."

So we all troop back in, and Joe says, "Okay, let's get this show on the road." And we start out. Joe kicks it off, and

I wish you could have seen the expression on the faces in the control booth. The major has the earphones on, and he's taking the earphones off and banging them, saying to the other fellow in the booth, "Can you hear anything?" And they've got these dials all set and they're flipping them around and going out of their minds trying to figure out why the sound's gone dead.

Meanwhile, a saxophone player is going through all these crazy contortions, looking like he was really playing a wild hot chorus, but, of course nothing was coming out. And then I got up and "sang" the chorus I was supposed to do, and I'd smile at them in the booth as if to say, "How's it coming through?" And the fellows are signaling: "Get closer! Get closer!"

Finally this major had banged his earphones so hard they fell apart — and they were completely wrecked. And the other guy had changed so many levers and everything, and two-and-a-half hours after we'd arrived there for rehearsal, they couldn't put that show on the air. They had just about torn up the whole control room.

Then Joe says, "Well, we can't stay any longer," and we left them, with everyone still working on the dials.

It was no more than the major deserved, but I've often felt sorry for those technicians and wondered whether they ever found out what was really the matter.

The Light Side of Jazz
Leonard Feather & Jack Tracy
Horizon Press, 1963. Reprinted from
New York: DeCapo Press 1979

CHAPTER TEN

Early American Music Humor

Americans tend to think of the 19th century as the bleak, dark, grim time of Civil War, with death from tuberculosis and other non-curable diseases. But life back then wasn't all that sad and bad. There was a light, upbeat tone to the period that was reflected in the humor of writers like Artemus Ward, Josh Billings and a host of others with a wonderful sense of humor and the ability to convey that, in the writer's own words.

What follows is a selection of humorous 19th and early 20th century stories dealing with music that reflect the humor of the time, from the phonetic spelling of Josh Billings to woefully exaggerated musical experiences. And all of it is quite funny — even today. See if you don't agree.

Song And Story

George Ade, 1931

As a further proof that the old-time saloon was the home of sentimental traditions and popular verse and harmonized choral effects, it is evident to any one that the humble citizen who has the urge to recite poetry or listen to folk-songs or be a rough second tenor in a close-harmony quartet that is tearing the lining out of "Way down yonder in the cornfield," now has absolutely no place to which he can go and blow off his stored-up emotions. Those who officiated at the carrying out of the death sentence against the liquor shops always insisted that the average workman or small-salaried minion who could not find an open bar-room would soon have more money in the savings bank and be enabled to pay the rent and provide the wife and children with clothes and shoes and show up on Monday morning without any cob-webs in the cranium and be a more efficient unit in the complicated machinery of production and distribution. The

Anti-Saloon League had nearly everything figured out except what the submerged poets and would-be Carusos were going to do with their evenings. The proletarian, often calling himself "the common dub," cannot join an expensive country club and help out on "Sweet Adeline" in the locker room. This hackneyed classic is nearly thirty years old, dating back to the later Lachrymose Period.

> "*In all my dreams,*
> *Your fair face beams.*"

This is almost a perfect specimen of the love-laden verse which was so popular in the saloons through the eighties and nineties and well into the present century. Once a prime favorite with the working classes, it is now an exclusive franchise controlled by the well-to-do. Those ominous rumblings in the ranks of organized labor come from mechanics and millhands, who feel that the Government had no right to take away from them not only their beer but also the chance to sing.

In one kind of place you could hear, "Wearin' of the Green," "The Harp that once through Tarra's Halls," "Where the River Shannon Flows," "You'll Never Find a Coward where the Shamrock Grows," and that heart-searching melody which is still popular whenever or wherever four men can get their heads together, "My Wild Irish Rose."

In another repository of Old World Memories the favorites might be "Hi-lee! Hilo!" "Ach du lieber Augustin," and "Die Wacht am Rhein." It was a dull evening which could not organize a Sangerfest.

But, in all of the places, during the gay nineties, when the slush-ma-gush ballads were in high favor, could have been heard the "Mother" songs and the recitals of insulted girlhood and betrayed womanhood. So far as vocal efforts were concerned, this period, which immediately pre-dated the beginning of the campaign against bar-drinking, was the saddest and most gushingly inconsequential of any in the history of the world.

It would seem that nowadays most of our popular songs are made up at the insane asylums, but a little before and after the Spanish-American War they seem to have originated either in undertaking parlors or the molasses factory.

H. T. Webster

On the desk is a great stock of the Delaney Song Books, published three times a year for many, many years. Probably the Delaney Co. gave up when it had to print nothing but boop-a-doop-doop and agonizing "blues." They perfected their type-setters against softening of the brain by closing down.

These Delaney paperback volumes contain the words only of songs which were in vogue and more or less admired on the various dates of publication. The early numbers are congested with tearful selections regarding "Mother." Only two songs regarding the male parent are now remembered — "Everybody Works but Father" and "The Old Man's Drunk Again."

It was William S. Gilbert, in the policemen's song of "The Pirates of Penzance," who remarked the baffling fact that when the coster wasn't "jumping on his mother," he was addicted to harmless fun. It is a true item of history that the lazy hulk of a loafer who paid no board at home and permitted his mother to chop the wood and bring in the coal was the one who broke down and wept like a child while listening to a maudlin tribute to "Dear Old Mother." The saloon harbored many low-grade characters, but the least estimate of the lot was the gorilla who cried over the sentimental songs. The most gentle-hearted buccaneers were those who scuttled ships. One of the never-ending surprises of Life is that always we are finding soft-heartedness where we least expect it. Al Capone, at Miami Beach one winter, deplored the fact that the newspapers were corrupting the youth of our fair land by making it appear that gangsters and racketeers were enjoying huge profits while immune from punishment!

You might think that the saloon, established for drinking purposes, would have specialized on convivial choruses which lauded the grape or the foaming tankard, but they did not go in for anything jolly. At a college reunion or yacht club dinner you could have heard something about a "stein on the table" and "a good old snifter of Hiram Walker." The sons of toil and the mercantile slaves who flocked to the bars every evening took their pleasures seriously and wallowed in the most abject sentimentality. They liked such things as the story of the bride who was "only a bird in a gilded cage," or the indignant waitress who informed the traveling salesman that her "mother was a lady," or of one who dwelt in "a mansion of aching hearts," or of the wayward girl whose picture had been turned "toward the wall" or of another lost soul who sent the following important message to her people:

> *"Just tell them that you saw me*
> *And they will know the rest."*

Their name was legion and all of them were weepy. They are as much out of style as low derby hats and puff sleeves but how real and beautiful they were to the emotional souses of yesterday! The ones about "Mother" predominated. Every nasal vocalist in the United States could render "A Boy's Best Friend Is His Mother." Another was called, "Always Take Mother's Advice," but the real heart-breaker was, "A Flower from My Angel Mother's Grave."

Let us rummage a little into the archives of the great Delaney and pick out a few that were typical. Even a fragment of each classic will give you some idea and help to convince you that the old-time saloon, instead of being a school for brutality, was an influence for the true, the beautiful and the good, especially about 11 p.m. with the bar-keep joining the group down near the ice-box and helping to hold the minors and the high notes.

In 1804 Dave Marion wrote one of the best, "Her Eyes Shine Like Diamonds," copyrighted by the Witmarks. The refrain concludes:

> *"With a smile she always greets me, from her I'll never*
> *part:*
> *For, lads, I love my mother and she's my sweetheart."*

It was in 1895 that the Witmarks published "Mother and Son," by Ellsworth. This is how the chorus started out:

> *"Never despair, dear mother, trust in our Father above,*
> *When you're sad, dear mother, think of your son and*
> *his love."*

Mention has been made of the one that all of them knew, "A Boy's Best Friend Is His Mother," evidently of British origin, because it was copyrighted away back in 1883 by T. B. Harms & Company of London. The chorus was one of the best:

> *"Then cherish her with care and smooth her*
> *silv'ry hair;*
> *When gone, you will never get another;*
> *And wherever we may turn, this lesson we will*
> *learn —*
> *A boy's best friend is his mother!"*

Joe Flynn, remembered by some of you, wrote "Little Hoop of Gold" in 1893, and it was copyrighted by the Witmarks. It rang with the kind of sentiment which was in fashion that year:

> *"Just a little band from my dear old mother's*
> *hand,*
> *Far dearer to me now than wealth untold;*
> *Though it's hardly worth a shilling,*
> *Still to die I would be willing,*
> *Ere I'd part with mother's little hoop of gold."*

These were just a few of a vast assortment. Possibly the words and music in defense of the rights of the working-man ranked third in popularity. First, the ones about dear old Mother; second, the ones about the poor girl who was tempted and who either fell or did not fall; third, the one about the organized workingmen and their nobility of character as compared with millionaire employers. I can find no printed copy of one I remember distinctly, and when I print it, I trust I am not disturbing any slumbering copyright:

> *"Your attention, friends I'll now invite,*
> *While I sing to you*
> *In regards to the cause of the working man*
> *Which, no doubt you'll find is true;*
> *For, the noble Knights of Labor*
> *Are doing the best they can*
> *To elevate the condition of*
> *The noble working man!"*

In the early nineties there was a favorite sketch in the variety halls called "Broadway swell and Bowery Bum."

Willie and Eugene Howard, of the present-day revues, have
a copy of the whole thing and will do it for you some time,
upon request. The songs and dialogue were copyrighted by
Frank Harding in 1892. The Broadway swell has no friendly
greeting for the friend of former days, who is now in tatters.
The bum, quoting from Bobby Burns, rebukes him as
follows:

> *"Although I'm but a working man, I live by*
>   *honest labor;*
> *I always do the best I can to assist a needy*
>   *neighbor;*
> *Content in health, is all my wealth, with*
>   *honesty to back it;*
> *My motives pure, although I'm poor, I respect*
>   *a ragged jacket."*

There you have the type of recitation which went over
with terrific success in any good bar-room. Every regular
place had a few patrons who spouted Shakespeare and had
some smattering of the classics. Of all the spoken pieces,
probably the most popular was the one by Burns to the
effect that "A man's a man for a' that." But there was another
standby which was worn threadbare before the boys got
through with it and, if you are not too young and knew the
history of your country, you have already guessed the title.
No large party, with all the faucets running, was complete
without "The Face on the Bar-room Floor." Many a reader,
when in a sentimental and reminiscent mood, could
undoubtedly recite that opening:

> *"'Twas a balmy summer evening and a goodly*
>   *crowd was there,*
> *Which well nigh filled Joe's bar-room, on the*
>   *corner of the square;*
> *And as songs and witty stories came through*
>   *the open door,*
> *A vagabond crept slowly in and posed upon*
>   *the floor."*

It ran through seventeen years and told about the boys
giving the vagabond many drinks and of his telling the story
of his life. He had been a great artist, with a beautiful wife,

whom he adored, but a handsome young friend stole her away and that was the beginning of his downfall. He borrows a piece of chalk and draws her angelic likeness on the bar-room floor and then falls over — dead! All very dramatic and with a perfect alcoholic finale. "The volunteer organist" and the tragic story of the destruction of the Newhall House in Milwaukee were in the repertoire of every two-handed drinker who aspired to be an elocutionist.

While we are talking about songs and recitations, it is worth noting that in all the Delaney books only one song can be found which seemed to put forward any plea for the saloon business and that was by Edward Harrigan and was in praise of the "Little Pitcher of Beer." Who doesn't remember the other kind — the songs which were directed against the "rum-shop" at every church entertainment and blue-ribbon celebration. The best remembered was the one beginning:

> *"Father, dear father, come home with me now,*
> *The clock in the steeple strikes one."*

Running a close second was the one about the little girl going into the saloon and singing as follows:

> *"Oh, Mr. Bartender, has father been here?*
> *He's not been at home all day —"*

Then there was the scathing one called "The Drunkard's Lone Child." It certainly didn't contain any kind words for the liquor trade, and it wound up as follows:

> *"Dark is the night, and the storm rages wild;*
> *God pity Bessie, the drunkard's lone child."*

These selections may help you to understand that the saloons did not do all of the sobbing. For some twenty years all of the school reciters and parlor soloists and male quartets just felt that they couldn't be artistic unless they featured grief, woe, misery, death and desolation. If the old-time saloon sounded the uttermost depths of disconsolation and melancholy it was because a keg of beer contained more weeps than a whole cistern full of rainwater.

257

"Do you mind if we sing just one Smith song?"

The First Piano in a Mining Camp

By Sam Davis

Mr. Samuel Davis was once a reporter for the San Francisco *Argonaut* and later the editor of the Carson *Appeal*. This story was written in 1885.

In 1858 — it might have been five years earlier or later; this is not the history for the public schools — there was a little camp about ten miles from Pioche, occupied by upwards of three hundred miners, every one of whom might have packed his prospecting implements and left for more inviting fields any time before sunset. When the day was over, these men did not rest from their labors, like the honest New England agriculturist, but sang, danced, gambled, and shot each other, as the mood seized them.

One evening, the report spread along the main street (which was the only street) that three men had been killed at

Silver Reef, and that the bodies were coming in. Presently a
lumbering old conveyance labored up the hill, drawn by a
couple of horses, well worn out with their pull. The cart contained a good-sized box, and no sooner did its outlines
become visible, through the glimmer of a stray light here and
there, than it began to affect the idlers. Death always
enforces respect, and even though no one had caught sight
of the reins, the crowd gradually became subdued, and
when the horses came to a stand-still, the cart was immediately surrounded. The driver, however, was not in the least
impressed with the solemnity of his commission.

"All there?" asked one.

"Haven't examined. Guess so."

The driver filled his pipe, and lit it as he continued:

"Wish the bones and load had gone over the grade!"

A man who had been looking on stepped up to the man
at once.

"I don't know who you have in that box, but if they happen to be any friends of mine, I'll lay you alongside."

"We can mighty soon see," said the teamster, coolly.
"Just burst the lid off, and if they happen to be the men you
want, I'm here."

The two looked at each other for a moment, and then
the crowd gathered a little closer, anticipating trouble.

"I believe that dead men are entitled to good treatment,
and when you talk about hoping to see corpses go over a
bank, all I have to say is, that it will be better for you if the
late lamented ain't my friends."

"We'll open the box. I don't take back what I've said,
and, if my language don't suit your ways of thinking, I guess
I can stand it."

With these words the teamster began to pry up the lid.
He got a board off, and then pulled out some old rags. A
strip of something dark, like rosewood, presented itself.

"Eastern coffins, by thunder!" said several, and the
crowd looked quite astonished.

Some more boards flew up, and the man who was ready
to defend his friend's memory shifted his weapon a little.
The cool manner of the teamster had so irritated him that he
had made up his mind to pull his weapon at the first sight of

the dead, even if the deceased was his worst and oldest enemy. Presently, the whole of the box cover was off, and the teamster, clearing away the packing, revealed to the astonished group the top of something which puzzled all alike.

"Boys," said he, "this is a pianner."

A general shout of laughter went up, and the man who had been so anxious to enforce respect for the dead, muttered something about feeling dry, and the keeper of the nearest bar was several ounces better off by the time the boys had given the joke all the attention it called for.

Had a dozen dead men been in the box, their presence in the camp could not have occasioned half the excitement that the arrival of that lonely piano caused. By the next morning, it was known that the instrument was to grace a hurdy-gurdy saloon, owned by Tom Goskin, the leading gambler in the place. It took nearly a week to get this wonder on its legs, and the owner was the proudest individual in the State. It rose gradually from a recumbent to an upright position amid a confusion of tongues, after the manner of the tower of Babel.

Of course, everybody knew just how such an instrument should be put up. One knew where the "off hind leg" should go, and another was posted on the "front piece."

Scores of men came to the place every day to assist.

"I'll put the bones in good order."

"If you want the wires tuned up, I'm the boy."

"I've got music to feed it for a month."

Another brought a pair of blankets for a cover, and all took the liveliest interest in it. It was at last in a condition for business.

"It's been showin' its teeth all the week. We'd like to have it spit out something."

Alas! There wasn't a man to be found who could play upon the instrument. Goskin began to realize that he had a loosing speculation on his hands. He had a fiddler, and a Mexican who thrummed a guitar. A pianist would have made his orchestra complete. One day, a three-card monte player told a friend confidentially that he could "knock any amount of music out of the piano, if he only had it alone a few hours, to get his hand in." This report spread about the camp, but on being questioned, he vowed that he didn't know a note of music. It was noted, however, as a suspicious circumstance, that he often hung about the instrument, and looked upon it longingly, like a hungry man gloating over a beefsteak in a restaurant window. There was no doubt but that this man had music in his soul, perhaps in his finger's ends, but did not dare to make trial of his strength after the rules of harmony had suffered so many years of neglect. So the fiddler kept on with his jigs, and the Mexican pawed his discordant guitar, but no man had the nerve to touch the piano. There were, doubtless, scores of men in the camp who would have given ten ounces of gold dust to have been half an hour alone with it, but every man's nerve shrank from the jeers which the crowd would shower upon him should his first attempt prove a failure. It got to be generally understood that the hand which first essayed to draw music from the keys must not slouch its work.

It was Christmas Eve, and Goskin, according to his custom, had decorated his gambling hall with sprigs of mountain cedar, and a shrub whose crimson berries did not seem a bad imitation of English holly. The piano was completely covered with evergreens, and all that was wanting to completely fill the cup of Goskin's contentment was a man to play the instrument.

"Christmas night, and no piano-pounder," he said. "This is a nice country for a Christian to live in."

Getting a piece of paper, he scrawled the words:

$20 Reward
To a compitant Pianer Player

This he stuck up on the music rack, and, though the inscription glared at the frequenters of the room until midnight, it failed to draw any musician from his shell.

So the merry-making went on; the hilarity grew apace. Men danced and sang to the music of the squeaky fiddle and worn-out guitar, as the jolly crowd within tried to drown the howling of the storm without. Suddenly they became aware of the presence of a white-haired man, crouching near the fire place. His garments — such as were left — were wet with melting snow, and he had a half-starved,

Giving them a rattle.

half-crazed expression. He held his thin, trembling hands toward the fire, and the light of the blazing wood made them almost transparent. He looked about him once in a while, as if in search of something, and his presence cast such a chill over the place that gradually the sound of the revelry was hushed, and it seemed that this waif of the storm had brought in with it, all of the gloom and coldness of the warring elements. Goskin, mixing up a cup of hot egg-nogg, advanced and remarked cheerily:

"Here, stranger, brace up! This is the real stuff."

The man drained the cup, smacked his lips, and seemed more at home.

"Been prospecting, eh? Out in the mountains — caught in the storm? Lively night this!"

"Pretty bad," said the man.

"Must feel pretty dry?"

The man looked at his streaming clothes and laughed as if Goskin's remark was a sarcasm.

"How long out?"

"Four days."

"Hungry?"

The man rose up, and walking over to the lunch counter, fell to work upon some roast bear, devouring it like any wild animal would have done. As meat and drink and warmth began to permeate the stranger, he seemed to expand and lighten up. His features lost their pallor, and he grew more and more content with the idea that he was not in the grave. As he underwent these changes, the people about him got merrier and happier, and threw off the temporary feeling of depression which he had laid upon them.

"Do you always have your place decorated like this?" he finally asked of Goskin.

"This is Christmas Eve," was the reply.

The stranger was startled.

"December twenty-fourth, sure enough."

"That's the way I put it up, pard."

"When I was in England, I always kept Christmas. But I had forgotten that this was the night. I've been wandering about in the mountains until I've lost track of the feasts of the church."

Presently his eye fell upon the piano.

"Where's the player?" he asked.

"Never had any," said Goskin, blushing at the expression.

"I used to play when I was young."

Goskin almost fainted at the admission.

"Stranger, do tackle it, and give us a tune! Nary man in this camp ever had the nerve to wrestle with the music-box." His pulse beat faster, for he feared that the man would refuse.

"I'll do the best I can," he said.

There was no stool, but seizing a candle-box, he drew it up and seated himself before the instrument. It only required a few seconds for a hush to come over the room.

"That old man is going to give the thing a rattle."

The sight of a man at the piano was something so unusual that even the faro dealer, who was about to take in a fifty-dollar bet on the trey, paused and did not reach for the money. Men stopped drinking, with the glasses at their lips.

Conversation appeared to have been struck with a sort of paralysis, and cards were no longer shuffled.

The old man brushed back his long white locks, looked up to the ceiling, half closed his eyes, and in a mystic sort of reverie, passed his fingers over the keys. He touched but a single note, yet the sound thrilled the room. It was the key to his improvisation, and as he wove his chords together, the music laid its spell upon every ear and heart. He felt his way along the keys, like a man treading uncertain paths; but he gained confidence as he progressed, and presently bent to his work like a master. The instrument was not in exact tune, but the ears of his audience, through long disuse, did not detect anything radically wrong. They heard a succession of grand chords, a suggestion of paradise, melodies here and there, and it was enough.

"See him counter with his left!" said an old rough, enraptured.

"He calls the turn every time on the upper end of the board," responded a man with a stack of chips in his hand.

The player wandered off into the old ballads they had heard at home. All the sad and melancholy and touching songs, that came up like dreams of childhood, this unknown player drew from the keys. His hands kneaded their hearts like dough, and squeezed out tears as from a wet sponge. As the strains flowed one upon the other, they saw their homes of the long ago reared again; they were playing once more where the apple blossoms sank through the soft air to join the violets on the green turf of the old New England States; they saw the glories of the Wisconsin maples and the haze of the Indian summer blending their hues together; they recalled the heather of Scottish hills, the white cliffs of Britain, and heard the sullen roar of the sea, as it beat upon their memories, vaguely. Then came all the old Christmas carols, such as they had sung in church thirty years before; the subtle music that brings up the glimmer of wax tapers, the solemn shrines, the evergreen, holly, mistletoe, and surpliced choirs. Then the remorseless performer planted his final stab in every heart with "Home Sweet Home."

Gone.

When the player ceased, the crowd slunk away from him. There was no more revelry and devilment left in his audience. Each man wanted to sneak off to his cabin and write the old folks a letter. The day was breaking as the last man left the place, and the player, laying his head down on the piano, fell asleep.

"I say, pard," said Goskin, "don't you want a little rest?"

"I feel tired," the old man said. "Perhaps you'll let me rest here for the matter of a day or so."

He walked behind the bar, where some old blankets were lying, and stretched himself upon them.

"I feel pretty sick. I guess I won't last long. I've got a brother down in the ravine — his name's Driscoll. He don't know I'm here. Can you get him before morning? I'd like to see his face once before I die."

Goskin started up at the mention of the name. He knew Driscoll well.

"He your brother? I'll have him here in half an hour."

As he dashed out into the storm, the musician pressed his hand to his side and groaned. Goskin heard the word

"Hurry!" and sped down the ravine to Driscoll's cabin. It was quite light in the room when the two men returned. Driscoll was pale as death.

"My God! I hope he's alive! I wronged him when we lived in England, twenty years ago."

They saw the old man had drawn the blankets over his face. The two stood a moment, awed by the thought that he might be dead. Goskin lifted the blanket, and pulled it down astonished. There was no one there!

"Gone!" cried Driscoll, wildly.

"Gone!" echoed Goskin, pulling out his cash drawer. "Ten thousand dollars in the sack, and the Lord knows how much loose change in the drawer!"

The next day, the boys got out, followed a horse's tracks through the snow and lost them in the trail leading towards Pioche.

There was a man missing from the camp. It was the three-card monte man, who used to deny point-blank that he could play the scale. One day, they found a wig of white hair, and called to mind when the "stranger" had pushed those locks back when he looked toward the ceiling for inspiration, on the night of December 24, 1858.

From *Mark Twain's and Other's
Library of Wit and Humor..* 1883

Show me a singing butterfly and I'll show you a humbug.

Jonathan at the Opera

From *Jonathan and His Continent*
Max O'rell and Jack Allyn. 1889

A Yankee in Paris — we mean an unadulterated, verdant, knotty specimen — is something of a curiosity. In the whirlpool of plaited trousers and sable mustaches, he looks like some remarkable nondescript that has got astray — the contrast is so great between your be-whiskered yellow

Frenchman and the long, gawky, Saxon-countenanced American. Throw a curiously carved chip on the bosom of the sea, and let it float far from the shores of civilization per- haps it will be picked up with a flood of wonderment. Set down on the dashing Boulevards, a raw, primitive, bony Vermonter, with no idea of society and the conventionalities of countries, and he will be as great an oddity as one could well conceive.

When we were in Paris last year, we encountered one of the latter class. He was disgracefully verdant, and had crossed the ocean to introduce a "scythe-sharpener," for which he had taken out a patent; but, according to his own account, everybody spoke so much French, he couldn't make them understand what he wanted to do. Of course, he had been sight-seeing, and had examined everything, from the antiques of the Louvre to the whirligig flourished on the Obelisk of Luxor, much to his gratification. After dinner one day, over the remains of a flacon of Bordeaux, he gave us a running account of his visit to the opera, which we will endeavor to transcribe, as nearly as possible, in his own words:

"The fact is," said he producing a pocket-knife, and a slip of wood as thick as an adult's forefinger, which he whit- tled with a dainty dexterity, "I come to France with an eye to biz'ness; and if I could pick up some crums of information, all well and good. But I've got a scythe-sharpener that beats everything that was ever invented clean out of the field — yes, far out of sight and gone! That's no braggin', on my honour. These Frenchman may be as ingenious as you please, but they can no more compare with the Yankees in agricultural things than you could expect to build an arsenal of duck eggs. I can make a scythe so desperate sharp that its shadow would be dangerous if you should run agin it in the dark; and as for the old system of whetting stones, the farmers in Vermont swear by me jist as the Turks did by Mohammed.

"But changin' the subject, this Paris is 'one of the places' now isn't it? Them Boo-le-vards are high old streets — beat Broadway and the Bowery all over! And that palace — what do you call it? — the Tweeleries — goes a-head of every-

thing I ever saw, except Buckin'ham Palace, where the
Queen boards in London. I went to the opera t'other night to
hear Albony — did you ever hear Albony sing. She's a jolly,
fat, comfortable-lookin' critter; but she's got a voice as sweet
as sugar, now, I tell you. Well, before I went to the opera,
somebody told me I must put on white kids and carry a
boquet. I up and said I would't, and then they allowed if I
did'nt, I could'nt git in; so as I wanted to hear Albony, I
thought I'd violate my conscience, and do it. I went to one
of them glove-shops in the Roo Pussinair, and a might slick-
lookin' gal — with her hair twisted like mint-sticks around her
head — fitted me with a pair, though I had a dreadful time to
make her understand what I wanted. I opinted first to my
hands, and she laughed and showed a double row of
ivories, and got down a gilt bottle with a label on it,
'Amandine,' or somethin' like that; but as I did'nt want no gilt
bottles, I shook my head, and made motions as if I was
pullin' on a glove, and at last she took the hint.

"I 'spose I must have split six pairs before I got one to fit;
and it would'nt have gone on at all if the gal had'nt coaxed
and rubbed it with her little white fingers. Talk about hands
— hers was lilies alongside of my great mallets! Well, after I
got the gloves, I had a deuce of a time before I could pay for
them. She couldn't make me understand how much they
were, non I could'nt make her explain clear enough; so I had
to end the matter by takin' out a handful of money, and lettin'
her help herself. Talk about uncomfortable people! I think I
was the greatest wretch in them gloves! It was the first pair
I ever had on in my life, and I walked about as if I had committed some dreadful sin.

"The next thing was to get a boquet; but as I could'nt see
one handy, I bought a bunch of water-cresses, and, mixin' a
dozen big stumpy scarlet radishes amongst 'em, I got my
ticket and walked in. Everybody stared at me, and feelin'
sassy, I stared back just as hard as they did. Lookin' up into
the gallery, I saw a passel of young chaps, all whiskers and
jewelry, pintin' at my boquet, and laughin' as if they'd tear
their mustaches. I look up two or three times, and made
mouths at 'em, but instead of their stoppin', it only made 'em
wus. And at last I got mad, and jerkin' off my kids with one

pull that ripped 'em as systematic as anything you ever saw,
I picked out the radishes from my bouquet, and commenced
firin' 'em at the bilious-lookin' wretches. Lord, how they
scattered! I knocked on feller's hat off, and it tumbled into
the pit. Another dropped his lorgn — the things they look
through to fetch the gals nearer — and three or four, in the
hurry to git out of the way, tripped over the back-benches,
and came sprawling on tew the floor.

"Three or four men rushed over to me, and spluttered
away somethin' in French; but they might as well have held
their tongues, for I could'nt make out a word they said. A
gentleman sittin' in the next box, who understood the
American language, translated what they said to me —
'They say you've broken the peace, and you must go out.'

"Tell 'em I won't do no sich thing. Those fellers laughed
at me, and I didn't pay my money to come in her to be snig-
gered at."

"He told 'em; but they told him back that I *must* leave, as
the audience were very much excited. Just then Albony
made her appearance, and waddled to music down to the
row of gas, and pitched her voice in a key that ought to have
restored quiet; but instead of doing so, everybody was taken
up with me, and bawled and squalled like a trunk full of
tom-cats.

"'Ho-o-o-o!' shouted the gallery.

"'Hi-i-i-i!' screeched the gallery.

"' Vo-o-o-o!' murmured the boxes.

"I saw then there was no use tryin' to stop where I was;
and gitting up to go, I found I had jist one radish left in my
boquet. I threw my eyes up to the gallery, and saw a long-
nosed cuss with a ruffled shirt, pintin' to me, and swearing'
like a trooper. I marked him well, and, drawin' off, I let go
the vegetable, and it took him alongside the head in a manner that made him have a singin' of the 'Marsallais' in his
ears, provided there was anything like tune in his body. This
kicked up a fresh excitement, for the fellow roared like a bull,
he was so mad, and I thought he would have slid down one
of the pillars to get at me.

"Before I could leave the boxes, three men pulled me by
the coat, mighty rough, and when I got into the lobby, I said

'Goodnight!' But I found they had no idea of partin' with me so soon; and the upshot of the whole thing was, that I had an escort to the police-office, where I was seated in company with a parcel of Johnny Darmes. Thinks I to myself, I might as well take this thing easy, and, so sendin' for a franes-woth of cigars, I treated the cocked hats all around, and we had a jolly time till morning.

"About twelve o'clock, I was taken before a squire — I reckon he was, only they don't call 'em squires here — and an interpreter asked me a hull procession of questions about who I was, where did I come from, and where I was goin'. I patted my own head, and said, after every one, 'Bon Amerique!' for that was about all of their confounded gibberish I knew. A passel of chaps in gowns and black inquisition-looking caps then put their noses together; and, in the end, they told the interpreter to tell me that it would cost twenty francs to once more get fresh air. I asked them to knock a little off, if they could manage it; but the judge, a dog-eyed man, squinted, mumbled somethin' to the lawyers, and I had to count out the money. Talk about French politeness! They didnt' as much as say, thank you for it, and I marched off with the determination that the next time I went to the opera to take no substitute for flowers, but get the real thing, if I had to go out of town and pluck 'em.

"Watercress boquets and radish-blossoms won't do in Paris!"

Little Patti
1862

Artemus Ward, 1834-1867

The moosic which Ime most use to is the inspirin stranes of the hand orgin. I hire a artistic Italyun to grind fur me, payin him his vittles & close & I spose it was them stranes which fust put a moosical taste into me. Like all furriners, he had seen better dase, havin formerly been a Kount. But he aint of much akount now, except to turn the orgin and drink Beer, of which bevrige he can hold a churnful, *easy*.

Miss Patty is small for her size, but as the man sed abowt his wife, O Lord! She is well bilt & her complexion is what might be called a Broonetty. Her ize is a dark bay, the lashes being long & silky. When she smiles the awjince feels like axing her to doo it sum moor, & to continner doing it 2 a indefnit extent. Her waste is one of the most bootiful wastisis ever seen. When Mister Strackhorse led her out I thawt sum pretty skool gal, who had jest graduatid frum pantalets & wire hoops, was a cumin out to read her fust composishun in public. She cum so bashful like, with her hed bowd down, & made sich a effort to arrange her lips so thayd look pretty, that I wanted to swaller her. She reminded me of Susan Skinner, who'd never kiss the boys at parin bees till the candles was blow'd out. Miss Patty sung suthin or ruther in a furrin tung. I don't know what the sentiments was. Fur awt I know she may hav bin denouncin my wax figger & sagashus wild beests of Pray, & I don't much keer ef she did. When she opened her mowth a army of martingales, bobolinks, kanarys, swallers, mockin birds, etsettery, bust 4th and flew all over the Haul.

Go it, little 1, sez I to myself, in a hily exsited frame of mind, & ef that kount or royal duke which you'll be pretty apt to marry 1 of these dase don't do the fair thing by ye, yu kin always hav a home on A. Ward's farm, near Baldinsville Injianny. When she sung Cumin three the Rye, and spoke of that Swayne she deerly luvd herself individooully, I didn't wish I was that air Swayne. No I gess not. Oh certainly not. [This is Ironical. I don't mean this. It's a way I hav of goakin.] Now that Maria Picklehoming has got married & left the perfeshun, Adeliny Patty is the championess of the opery ring. She karries the Belt. That's no draw fite about it. Other primy donnys may as well throw up the spunge first as last. My eyes don't deceive my earsite in this matter.

But Miss Patty orter sing in the Inglish tung. As she kin do so as well as she kin in Italynn, why under the Son don't she do it? What cents is thare in singin wurds nobody don't understan when wurds we do understan is jest as handy. Why peple will versifferusly applawd furrin langwidge is a mistery. It reminds me of a man I onct knew. He sed he knockt the bottum out of his pork Barril, & the pork fell out,

but the Brine dident moove a inch. It stade in the Barril. He
sed this was a Mistery, but it wasn't misterior than is this
thing I'm speekin of.

As fur Brignoly, Ferri and Junky, they air dowtless grate,
but I think sich able boddied men wood look better tillin the
sile than dressin theirselves up in black close & white kid
gluvs & shoutin in a furrin tung. Mister Junky is a noble
lookin old man, & orter lead armies on the Battel instid of
shoutin in a furrin tung.

Adoo. In the langwidge of Lewis Napoleon when
receivin kumpany at his pallis on the Bullyvards, "I saloot
yu."

Before Pa got tuned in on jazz!

Josh Billings (Henry Wheeler Shaw) 1818-1888, was
the pre-eminent, 19th century American humorist. He was
the beloved "funny man" of Abraham Lincoln, who said of
him: "Josh Billings is the best judge of human nature since
Shakespeare."

He writes his humor with phonetic spelling—a popular
humor mode of his day and today. Readers may find it
takes a little time to adjust to its ungrammaticalness, but
Josh Billings still is as funny as he was 150 years ago, phonetic spelling not withstanding.

Whissling

Josh Billings
Hiz Sayings 1865

I hav spent a grate deal ov sarching, and sum money, tew find out who waz the first whissler, but up tew now I am just az mutch uncivilized on the subjekt as I was.

I kan tell who played on the first juice harp, and who beat the fust tin pan, and I kno the year the harp ov a thousand strings waz diskovered in, but when whissling waz an infant, iz az hard for me tew say, az mi prayers in lo dutch.

Whissling.

Whissling iz a wind instrument, and iz did bi puckring up the mouth, and blowing through the hole.

Thare aint no tune on the whole earth but what kan be played on this instrument, and that selebrated old tune, Yankeedoodle haz bin almost whissled tew deth.

Grate thinkers are not apt tew be good whisslers, in fakt, when a man kant think ov nother, then he begins tew whissell. We seldom see a raskal who iz a good whissler, thare iz a grate deal ov honor bright, in a sharp, well–puckered whissell.

Good whisslers are gitting skarse, 75 years ago they waz plenty, but the desire tew git ritch, or tew hold offiss, haz took the pucker out ov this honest and cheerful amuzement.

If I had a boy, who couldn't whissell, I don't want tew be understood, that I should feel at liberty, tew giv the boy up for lost, but I would mutch rather he would kno how tew whissell fust rate, than to know how tew play a seckord rate game ov kards.

273

I wouldn't force a boy ov mine tew whissell agin his natral inclinashun.

Wimmin az a kind, or in the lump, are poor whizzlers, I don't know how I found this out, but I am glad ov it, it iz a good deal like crowing in a hen.

Crowing iz an unladylike thing in a hen tew do.

I hav often heard hens tri tew cro, but I never knuw one tew do herself justiss.

A rooster kan krow well, and a hen kan kluk well, and I sa let each one ov them stik tew their trade.

Klucking iz kist az necessary in this wurld az crowing espeshily if it iz well did.

But I want it well understood that I am the last man on reckord who would refuse a woman a chance tew whissell if she waz certain she had the right pucker for it.

I never knu a good whissler but what had a good consti-tution. Whissling iz compozed ov pucker and wind, and these two accomplishments denote vigor.

Sum people alwus whissel whare thare iz danger—this they do to keep the fraid out ov them. When I waz a boy I alwus konsidered whissling the next best thing to a kandle to go down cellar with in the nite time.

I don't want enny better evidence ov the general honesty thare iz in a whissel than the fackt that thare aint nothing which a dog will answer quicker than the wizzell ov hiz mas-ter, and dogs are az good judges ov honesty az enny kritters that live.

It iz hard work to phool a dog once, and it iz next to impossible to phool him the sekond time.

I aint afraid to trust enny man for a small amount who iz a good whissler.

I wouldn't want to sell him a farm on credit, for I should expekt to hav to take the farm back after awhile and remove the mortgage miself.

Yu cant whissell a mortgage oph from a farm.

A fust rate whissler iz like a middling sized fiddler, good for nothing else, and tho whissling may keep a man from git-ting lonesum, it wont keep him from gitting ragged.

I never knu a bee hunter but what waz a good whissler, and I don't kno ov enny bizzness on the breast ov the earth that will make a man so lazy and useless, without acktually killing him, az hunting bees in the wilderness.

Hunting bees and writing seckond rate verses are evidences ov sum genious, but either of them will unfit a man for doing a good square day's work.

An Essa Onto Musik

Josh Billings
Hiz Sayings - 1865
*"Musick hath charms to sooth a savage.
To rend a rok or split a kabbage"*

So tha tell me, but I shud rather try a revolver on the savage, a blast ov powder on the rok, and good sharp vinegar on the kabbage. I haint searched history tew diskiver who giv the first consert ov musik. We are told, that in *those days* "the stars sang together," but in *theze days* yu knt git stars tew sing together. We often hear it said, "that such a person haz a good ear for musik," I don't fellership this remark; awl a person wants tew understand musik with, is a good soul; a "good ear" haint got enny more tew du with it than a good sett ov brains has tu do with charity. Musical crickets insists that if the gammut aint rite, the musik aint rite; this is awl nonsense; the gammut haint got enny more tew du with a musick-hungry man, than a knife and fork has with his dinner, if he is real hungry he can eat with his fingers. Musick want got up tew make us wise, but better natured. How much opera musick dew you suppose it wud taik tu make a man cry? Folks will tell yu that such an "overture fria dabulo" (or sum uther furrin being named thing) "waz moste heavenly rendered," tha mite as well tell me that a pumpkin pie was heavenly rendered. What do I care about the rendering, if I don't git a piece ov the pie? Let some Prime Donner, or Mezzer Soapraner, or Barrytown Base or some sich latin individual, cum into this village, and histe their flag, and have a programmy ov singing as long as a sarch warrant, and as hard tu spell out as a chinese proklamashun ritten upside down, and taxed seventy-five cents for a preserved seat, and moste evrybody will go tu hear it, bekause moste everybody else dus, and will sa evry now and then, (out loud) "How bewitching! How delishus! How egstatick!" and nineteen out ov evry twenty-one ov them wouldn't kno if the performance was a burlesk on their grandmother. Wouldn't it be fun tew cee one ov these opera singers undertake tu rok a baby tu sleep? I gess thare wud be two parts carried tu that song about that time. Suppose yu shud come home at nite, a weary boy, and la yure hed in mother's lap, and she shud let out a opera, good Lord! wouldn't yu think yure mother was a lunatik, or ought to be one at onst, tu save her karacter. "Korrect taist," iz anuther big wurd; ive herd folks uze it whose finger nales wanted cleaning. Musik, after all, is sumthing like vittels, the more cooking and seasoning we use, the more we hav to hav, till after awhile we kant enjoy ennything ov the vittels but the pepper. Opera don't hav enny more loosening affeck on me, that caster ile wud on a graven image. I set and gaze, and hark, and cee the whole aujence in hirogliphicks, and awl I can do iz tu git mad that sich stuff is called musik. But awl the reasoning in the wurld wont convince menny people that haint got a rite tew go into fits over an opera tha don't understand a word ov; it iz the fashion tew expire and have their souls dissolve in latin at the rate ov seventy-five cents, and it haz got to be did, "sink or swim, survive or perish." If enny boddy wants tu go and hear a man or woman disgorge musick, that has more kolik than melody into it, I supose (under the constiushun) tha hav jist the same rite tew crusifi themselves enny uther way, for sumbody's else sins that tha don't know the natur of.

The Harp of a Thousand Strings

William Penn Brannon
From *The Harp of a Thousand Strings*; or, *Laughter for a Lifetime*...Konceived, Compiled and Komically Konkokted by Spavery [S. P. Avery?], New York: Dick & Fitzgerald, Publishers, 1858

... "That may be some here to-day, my brethering, as don't know what persuasion I am uv. Well, I may say to you, my brethering, that I am a Hard-Shell Baptist. Thar's some folks as don't like the Hard-Shell Baptists, but I'd rather hev a hard shell as no shell at all. You see me here to-day, my brethering, dressed up in fine close; you might think I was proud, but I am not proud, my brethering; and although I've been a preacher uv the gospel for twenty years, and although I'm capting uv that flat-boat that lies at your land-ing, I'm not proud, my brethering.

"I'm not gwine ter tell you *edzackly* whar my tex may be found: suffice it tu say, it's in the leds of the Bible, and you'll find it somewhar 'tween the fust chapter of the book of Generation, and the last chapter of the book of Revolutions, and ef you'll go and sarch the Scripturs, you'll not only find *my* tex thar, but a great many other *texes* as will do you good to read; and my tex, when you shill find it, you shill find it to read thus:

"'And he played on a harp uv a thousand strings — sperits of just men made perfeck.'

"My tex, brethren, leads me to speak uv sperits as is ment in the tex: it's *fire*. That is the kind of sperits as is ment in the tex, my brethering. Now thar's a great many kinds of fire in the world. In the fust place, thar's the com-mon sort uv fire you light a segar or pipe with, and then thar's fire, for the tex ses: 'He played on a harp uv a *thou*-sand strings — sperits uv just men made perfeck.'

"But I'll tell you the kind of fire as is ment in the tex, my brethering — it's *hell-fire*! An' that's the kind of fire as a great many of you'll come to, ef you don't do better nor what you have bin doing' — for 'He played on a harp uv a *thou*-sand strings — sperits of just men made perfeck.'

"Now, the different sorts uv fire in the world may be likened unto the different persuasions in the world. In the first place, we have the 'Piscapalions, and they are a high salin' and a highfalutin' set, and they may be likened unto a turkey-buzzard, that flies up into the air, and he goes up and up till he looks no bigger than your finger-nail, and the fust thing you know, he comes down and down, and is a fillin' himself on the karkiss of a dead hoss by the side uv the road — and 'He played on a harp uv a *thou*-sand strings — sperits of just men made perfeck.'

"And then, thar's the Methodis, and they may be likened unto the squirrel, runnin' up into a tree, for the Methodis believes in gwine on from one degree uv grace to another, and finally on to perfecshun; and the squirrel goes up and up, and he jumps from lim' to lim', and branch to branch, and the fust thing you know, he falls, and down he comes kerflummux' and that's like the Methodis, for they is allers fallin' from Grace, ah! And 'He played on a part of a *thou*-sand strings — sperits of just men made perfeck.'

"And then, my brethering, thar's the Baptist, ah! And they hev bin likened unto a possum on a 'simmon tree, and the thunders may roll, and then the earth may quake, but that possum clings there still, ah! And you may shake one foot loose, and the other's thar; and you may shake all feet loose, and he laps his tail around the lim', and he clings fur ever — for 'He played on a harp of a *thou*-sand strings — sperits of just men make perfeck.'"

"If you want to make old Satan run,
    Play on the golden harp!
Just shoot him with the gospel gun,
    Play on the golden harp!
Play on the golden harp! Play on the golden harp!

Musical Review Extraordinary

John Phoenix, 1856

San Diego, July 10th, 1854. As your valuable work is not supposed to be so entirely identified with San Franciscan interests, as to be careless what takes place in other portions of this great *kedntry*, and as it is received and read in San Diego with great interest (I have loaned my copy to over four different literary gentlemen, most of whom have read some of it), I have thought it not improbable that a few critical notices of the musicical performances and the drama of this place might be acceptable to you, and interest your readers. I have been, moreover, encouraged to this task by

the perusal of your interesting musical and theatrical critiques on San Francisco performers and performances; as I
feel convinced that, if you devote so much space to them,
you will not allow any little feeling of rivalry between the two
great cities to prevent your noticing ours, which, without the
slightest feeling of prejudice, I must consider as infinitely
superior. I propose this month to call your attention to the
two great events in our theatrical and musical world — the
appearance of the talented MISS PELICAN, and the production of Tarbox's celebrated "Ode Symphonie" or "The
Plains."

The critiques on the former are from the columns of *The
Vallecetos Sentinel*, to which they were originally contributed
by me, appearing on the respective dates of June 1st and
June 31st.

From The Vallecetos Sentinel, *June 1st.*

MISS PELICAN. — Never during our dramatic experience, has a more exciting event occurred than the sudden
bursting upon our theatrical firmament, full, blazing, unparal-
leled, of the bright, resplendent and particular star, whose
honored name shines refulgent at the head of this article.
Coming among us unheralded, almost unknown, without
claptrap, in a wagon drawn by oxen across the plains, with
no agent to get up a counterfeit enthusiasm in her favor, she
appeared before us for the first time at the San Diego
Lyceum, last evening, in the trying and difficult character of
Ingomar, or the Tame Savage. We are at a loss to describe
our sensations, our admiration, at her magnificent, her
superhuman efforts. We do not hesitate to say that she is
by far the superior of any living actress; and, as we believe
hers to be the perfection of acting, we cannot be wrong in
the belief that no one hereafter will ever be found to
approach her. Her conception of the character of Ingomar
was perfection itself; her playful and ingenuous manner, her
light girlish laughter, in the scene with Sir Peter, showed an
appreciation of the savage character, which nothing but the
most arduous study, the most elaborate training could produce; while her awful change to the stern, unyielding,
uncompromising father in the tragic scene of Duncan's mur-

der, was indeed nature itself. Miss Pelican is about seventeen years of age, of miraculous beauty, and most thrilling voice. It is needless to say she dresses admirably, as in fact we have said all we can say when we called her most truthfully, perfection. Mr. John Boots took the part of Parthenia very creditably, etc., etc.

From The Vallecetos Sentinel, *June 31st.*

MISS PELICAN. — As this lady is about to leave us to commence an engagement on the San Francisco stage, we should regret exceedingly if any thing we have said about her, should send with her a *prestige* which might be found undeserved on trial. The fact is, Miss Pelican is a very ordinary actress; indeed, one of the most indifferent ones we ever happened to see. She came here from the Museum at Fort Laramie, and we praised her so injudiciously that she became completely spoiled. She has performed a round of characters during the last week, very miserably, though we are bound to confess that her performance of King Lear last evening, was superior to any thing of the kind we ever saw. Miss Pelican is about forty-three years of age, singularly plain in her personal appearance, awkward and embarrassed, with a cracked and squeaking voice, and really dresses quite outrageously. *She has much to learn — poor thing!*

I take it the above notices are rather ingenious. The fact is, I'm no judge of acting, and don't know how Miss Pelican will turn out. If well, why there's my notice of June the 1st; if ill, then June 31st comes in play, and, as there is but one copy of the *Sentinel* printed, it's an easy matter to destroy the incorrect one; *both can't be wrong*, so I've made a sure thing of it in any event. Here follows my musical critique, which I flatter myself is of rather superior order:

THE PLAINS. ODE SYMPHONIE PAR JABEZ TARBOX. — This glorious composition was produced at the San Diego Odeon, on the 31st of June, ult., for the first time in this or any other country, by a very full orchestra (the performance taking place immediately after supper), and a chorus composed of the entire "Sauer Kraut-Verein," the "Wee

Gates Association," and choice selections from the
"Gyascutus" and "Pikeharmonic" societies. The solos were
rendered by Herr Tuden Links, the recitations by Herr Von
Hyden Schnapps, both performers being assisted by
Messrs. John Smith and Joseph Brown, who held their
coats, fanned them, and furnished water during the more
overpowering passages.

"The Plains" we consider the greatest musical achieve-
ment that has been presented to an enraptured public. Like
Waterloo among battles; Napoleon among warriors;
Niagara among falls, and Peck among senators, this magnificent composition stands among Oratorios, Operas, Musical
Melodramas and performances of Ethiopian Serenaders,
peerless and unrivalled: *Il frappe toute chose parfaitment
froid.*

"It does not depend for its success" upon its plot, its
theme, its school or its master, for it has very little if any of
them, but upon its soul-subduing, all-absorbing, high-faluting
effect upon the audience, every member of which it causes
to experience the most singular and exquisite sensations.
Its strains at times remind us of those of the old master of
the steamer *McKim*, who never went to sea without being
unpleasantly affected; — a straining after effect he used to
term it. Blair in his lecture on beauty, and Mills in his trea-
tise on logic (p. 31), have alluded to the feeling which might
be produced in the human mind, by something of this tran-
scendentally sublime description, but it has remained for M.
Tarbox, in the production of "the Plains," to call this feeling
forth.

The symphonie opens upon the wide and boundless
plains, in longitude 115° W., latitude 35° 21′ 03″ N., and
about sixty miles from the west bank of Pitt River. These
data are beautifully and clearly expressed by a long (topo-
graphically) drawn note from an E-flat clarionet. The sandy
nature of the soil, sparsely dotted with bunches of cactus
and artemisia, the extended view, flat and unbroken to the
horizon, save by the rising smoke in the extreme verge,
denoting the vicinity of a Pi Utah village, are represented by
the bass drum A few notes on the piccolo, calls the attention to a solitary antelope, picking up mescal beans in the

281

foreground. The sun having an altitude of 36º 27′, blazes down upon the scene in indescribable majesty, "Gradually the sounds roll forth in a song" of rejoicing to the God of Day.

> "Of thy intensity
> And great immensity
>   Now then we sing;
> Beholding in gratitude
> Thee in this latitude,
>   Curious thing."

Which swells out into "Hey Jim along, Jim along Josey," then *decrescendo, mas o menos, poco pocita*, dies away and dries up.

Suddenly we hear approaching a train from Pike County, consisting of seven families, with forty-six wagons, each drawn by thirteen oxen; each family consists of a man in butternut-colored clothing driving the oxen; a wife in butternut-clothing riding in the wagon, holding a butternut baby, and seventeen butternut children running promiscuously about the establishment; all are barefooted, dusty, and smell unpleasantly. (All these circumstances are expressed by pretty rapid fiddling for some minutes, winding up with a puff from the orpheclide, played by an intoxicated Teuton with an atrocious breath — it is impossible to misunderstand the description.) Now rises o'er the plains in mellifluous accents, the grand Pike County Chorus.

> "Oh, we'll soon be thar
> In the land of gold,
> Through the forest old,
> O'er the mounting cold,
> With spirits bold —
> Oh, we come, we come,
> And we'll soon be thar.
>   Gee up Bolly! Whoo, up, whoo haw!

The train now encamps. The unpacking of the kettles and mess-pans, the unyoking of the oxen, the gathering about the various camp-fires, the frizzling of the pork, are so clearly expressed by the music, that the most untutored savage could readily comprehend it. Indeed, so vivid and life-like was the representation, that a lady sitting near us, involuntarily exclaimed aloud, at a certain passage, "*Thar, that pork's burning!*" and it was truly interesting to watch the gratified expression of her face when, by a few notes of the guitar, the pan was removed from the fire, and the blazing pork extinguished.

This is followed by the beautiful *aria*: —

"O! marm, I want a pancake!"

Followed by that touching *recitative*: —

"Shet up, or I will spank you!"

To which succeeds a grand *crescendo* movement, representing the flight of the child, with the pancake, the pursuit of the mother, and the final arrest and summary punishment of the former, represented by the rapid and successive strokes of the castanet.

The turning in for the night follows; and the deep and stertorous breathing of the encampment, is well given by the bassoon, while the sufferings and trials of an unhappy father with an unpleasant infant, are touchingly set forth by the *cornet à piston*.

Part Second — The night attack of the Pi Utahs; the fearful cries of the demoniac Indians; the shrieks of the females and the children; the rapid and effective fire of the rifles; the stampede of the oxen; their recovery and the final repulse; the Pi Utahs being routed after a loss of thirty-six killed and wounded, while the Pikes lose but one scalp (from an old fellow who wore a wig, and lost it in the scuffle), are faithfully given, and excite the most intense interest in the minds of the hearers; the emotions of fear, admiration and delight, succeeding each other in their minds, with almost painful rapidity. Then follows the grand chorus:

"Oh! We gin them fits,

The Ingen Utahs.

With our six-shooters —

We gin 'em pertickuler fits."

After which, we have the charming recitative of Herr Tuden Links, to the infant, which is really one of the most charming gems in the performance:

"Now, dern your skin, *can't* you be easy?"

Morning succeeds. The sun rises magnificently (octavo flute) — breakfast is eaten, — in a rapid movement on three sharps; the oxen are caught and yoked up — with a small drum and triangle; the watches, purses, and other valuables of the conquered Pi Utahs, are stored away in a camp-kettle, to a small movement on the piccolo, and the train moves on, with the grand chorus: —

"We'll soon be thar,
  Gee up Bolly! Whoo hup! Whoo haw!"

The whole concludes with the grand hymn and
  chorus: —

"When we die we'll go up to Benton,
  Whup! Whoo, haw!
The greatest man that e'er land saw,
  Gee!
Who this little airth was sent on
  Whup! Whoo, haw!
To tell a 'hawk from a hand-saw!'
  Gee!"

The immense expense attending the production of this magnificent work; the length of time required to prepare the chorus; the incredible number of instruments destroyed at each rehearsal, have hitherto prevented M. Tarbox from placing it before the American public, and it has remained for San Diego to show herself superior to her sister cities of the Union, in musical taste and appreciation, and in high-souled liberality, by patronizing this immortal prodigy, and enabling its author to bring it forth in accordance with his wishes and its capabilities. We trust every citizen of San Diego and Vallecetos will listen to it ere it is withdrawn; and if there yet lingers in San Francisco one spark of musical fervor, or a remnant of taste for pure harmony, we can only say that the *Southerner* sails from that place once a fortnight, and that the passage money is but forty-five dollars.

How Rubenstein Played

George Bagby, 1850
From *The Old Virginia Gentlemen and Other Sketches*
The following was offered originally to *The Philadelphia Weekly Times*, but declined on the ground that "Rubenstein

is no longer in this country." Gillis printed it in *The Richmond Sunday Transcript*, paying nothing for it, and it made no noise here. But soon it was copied all over the country in newspapers and selections for Humorous Readings without the author's name. It has been read in public by Willoughby Reade, myself and others and has proved to be the most popular piece I ever wrote.

              Author's note.

 "Jud, they say you heard Rubenstein play when you were in New York."

  "I did, in the cool."

  "Well, tell us about it."

  "What! Me? I might's well tell you about the creation of the world."

  "Come, now; no mock modesty. Go ahead."

  "Well, Sir, he had the blamedest, biggest, catty-cornedest pianner you ever laid eyes on; somethin' like a distractid billiard table on three legs. The lid was heisted, and mighty well it was. If it hadn't been he'd a-tore the intire insides clean out, and scattered 'em to the four winds of heaven."

  "Played well, did he?"

  "You bet he did; but don't interrup' me. When he first set down he 'peard to keer mighty little 'bout playin', and wished he hadn' come. He tweedle-leedled a little on the trible, and twoodle-oodle-oodled some on the base — just foolin' and boxin' the thing's jaws for bein' in his way. And I says to a man settin' next to me, s'I, 'what sort of fool playin' is that?' And he says, 'Heish!' But presently his hands commenced chasin' one 'nother up and down the keys, like a passel of rats scamperin' through a garret very swift. Parts of it was sweet, though, and reminded me of a sugar squirrel turnin' the wheel of a candy cage.

  "'Now,' I says to my neighbor, 'he's showin' off. He thinks he's a doing of it; but he ain't got no idee, no plan of nuthin'. If he'd play me up a tune of some kind or other, I'd —'

  "But my neighbor says 'Heish!' very impatient.

  "I was just about to git up and go home, bein' tired of that foolishness, when I heard a little bird waking up away off in the woods, and calling sleepy-like to his maté, and I looked up and I see that Ruben was beginnin' to take some interest in his business, and I set down agin. It was the peep o' day. The light come faint from the east, the breeze blowed gentle and fresh, some more birds waked up in the orchard, then some more in the trees near the house, and all begun singin' together. People begun to stir, and the gal opened the shutters. Just then the first beam of the sun fell upon the blossoms; a leetle more and it tetcht the roses on the bushes, and the next thing it was broad day; the sun fairly blazed; the birds sang like they'd split their little throats; all the leaves was movin', and flashin' diamonds of dew, and the whole wide world was bright and happy as a king. Seemed to me like there was a good breakfast in every house in the land, and not a sick child or woman any-where. It was a fine mornin'.

"And I says to my neighbor, 'That's music, that is.'

"But he glar'd at me like he'd like to cut my throat.

"Presently the wind turned; it begun to thicken up, and a kind of gray mist come over things; I got low-spirited d'rect-ly. Then a silver rain began to fall. I could see the drops touch the ground; some flashed up like long pearl ear-rings, and the rest rolled away like round rubies. It was pretty, but melancholy. Then the pearls gathered themselves into long strands and necklaces, and then they melted into thick silver streams running between golden gravels, and then the streams joined each other at the bottom of the hill, and made a brook that flowed silent except that you could kinder see the music, specially when the bushes on the banks moved as the music went along down the valley. I could smell the flowers in the meadow. But the sun didn't shine, nor the birds sing; it was a foggy day, but not cold. The most curious thing was the little white angel boy, like you see in pictures, that run ahead of the music brook, and led it on, and on, away out of the world, where no man ever was — *I* never was, certain. I could see that boy just as plain as I see you. Then the moonlight came, without any sunset, and shone on the grave-yards, where some few ghosts lifted their hands and went over the wall, and between the black sharp-top trees splendid marble houses rose up, with fine ladies in the lit up windows, and men that loved 'em, but could never get a-nigh 'em, and played on guitars under the trees, and made me that miserable I could a-cried, because I wanted to love somebody, I don't know who better than the men with guitars did. Then the sun went down, it got dark, the wind moaned and wept like a lost child for its dead mother, and I could a got up then and there and preached a better sermon than any I ever listened to. There wasn't a thing in the world left to live for, not a blame thing, and yet I didn't want the music to stop one bit. It was happier to be miserable than to be happy without being miserable. I couldn't understand it. I hung my head and pulled out my hankerchief, and blowed my nose loud to keep from cryin'. My eyes is weak anyway; I didn't want anybody to be a-gazin' at me a-snivlin', and its nobody's business what I do with my nose, It's mine. But some several glared at me, mad as Tucker.

"Then, all of a sudden, old Ruben changed his tune. He ripped and he rar'd, he tipped and tar'd, he pranced and he charged like the grand entry at a circus. 'Peared to me that all the gas in the house was turned on at once, things got so bright, and I hilt up my head, ready to look any man in the face, and no afeard of nothin'. It was a circus, and a brass band, and a big ball, all goin' on at the same time. He lit into them keys like a thousand of brick, he give 'em no rest, day nor night; he set every livin' joint in me a-going', and not bein' able to stand it no longer, I jumpt spang onto my seat, and jest hollored:

"'*Go it, my Rube!*'

"Every blamed man, woman and child in the house riz on me, and shouted, 'Put him out! Put him out!'

"Put your great-grandmother's grizzly-gray-greenish cat into the middle of next month!' I says. "Tech me, if you dare! I paid my money, and you jest come a-nigh me.'

"With that, some several p'licemen run up, and I had to simmer down. But I would a fit any food that laid hands on me, for I was bound to hear Ruby out or die.

"He had changed his tune again. He hopt-light ladies and tip-toed fine from eend to eend of the keyboard. He played soft, and low, and solemn. I heard the church bells over the hills. The candles in heaven was lit, one by one. I saw the stars rise. The great organ of eternity began to play from the world's end to the world's end, and all the angels went to prayers. Then the music changed to water, full of feeling that couldn't be thought, and began to drop — drip, drop, drip, drop — clear and sweet, like tears of joy fallin' into a lake of glory. It was sweeter than that. It was as sweet as a sweetheart sweetenin' sweetness with white sugar, mixt with powdered silver and seed diamonds. It was too sweet. I tell you the audience cheered. Ruben he kinder bowed, like he wanted to say, 'Much obleeged, but I'd rather you wouldn't interrup' me.'

He stopped a moment or two to catch breath. Then he got mad. He run his fingers through his hair, he shoved up his sleeve, he opened his coat tails a little further, he drug up his stool, he leaned over, and Sir, he jest went for that old pianner. He slapped her face, he boxed her jaws, he pulled her nose, he pinched her ears, and he scratched her cheeks, until she fairly yelled. She bellered like a bull, she bleated like a calf, she howled like a hound, she squealed like a pig, she shrieked like a rat, and *then* he wouldn't let her up. He run a quarter stretch down the low grounds of the bass, till he got clean in the bowels of the earth, and you heard thunder galloping after thunder, through the hollows and cases of perdition. Then he fox-chased his right hand with his left till he got way out of the treble into the clouds, where the notes was finer than the points of cambrick needles, and you couldn't hear nothing but the shadders of 'em.

And then he wouldn't let the old pianner go. He forward two'd, he crossed over first gentleman, he sashayed right and left, back to your places, he all hands'd round, ladies to the right, promenade all, here and there, back and forth, up and down, perpetual motion, double, twisted and turned and tacked and tangled into forty-eleven thousand double bow knots.

By jinks, it was a mixtery! He fetched up his right wing, he fetched up his left wing, he fetch up his centre, he fetched up his reserves. He fired by file, he fired by platoons, by company, by regiments and by brigades. He opened his cannon, siege guns down thar, Napoleons here, twelve-pounders yonder, big guns, little guns, middle-size guns, round shot, shell, shrapnel, grape, canister, mortars, mines and magazines, every livin' battery and bomb a-goin' at the same time. The house trembled, the lights danced, the walls shuk, the floor come up, the ceilin' come down, the sky split, the ground rockt — heavens and earth, creation sweet potatoes, Moses, nine-pences, glory ten-penny nails, my Mary Ann, hallelujah, Samson in a 'simmon tree, Jeroosal'm, Tump Tompson in a tumbler-cart, roodle-oodle-oodle-oodle — ruddle-uddle-uddle-uddle — raddle, addle, addle, addle, addle — riddle-iddle-iddle-iddle — reetle-eetle-eetle-eetle-eetle-eetle — p-r-r-r-r-r-lang! Per lang! Per plang! P-r-r-r-r-r-r-lang! Bang!

"With that *bang!* he lifted hisself bodily into the a'r, and he come down with his knees, his ten fingers, his ten toes, his elbows and his nose, striking every single solitary key on that pianner at the same time. The thing busted and went off into seventeen hundred and fifty-seven thousand five hundred and forty-two hemi-demi-semi-quivers, and I know'd no mo'.

"When I come too, I were under ground about twenty foot, in a place they call Oyster Bay, treatin' a Yankee that I never laid eyes on before, and never expect to ag'in. Day was a breakin' by the time I got to the St. Nicholas Hotel, and I pledge you my word I didn't know my name. The man asked me the number of my room, and I told him, *'Hot music on the half-shell for two!'* I pintedly did."

Show me a bunch of beggars and I'll show you a ragtime band.

Show me a violin maker and I'll show you a guy with guts.

We always missed the last half of the last act when the girls started to put their hats on.

Reprinted with permission by The Chicago Tribune

Slavin Contra Wagner

Finley Peter Dunne
Mr. Dooley's in the Hearts of His Countrymen, 1899

"Ol' man Donahue bought Molly a pianny las' week," Mr. Dooley said in the course of his conversation with Mr. McKenna. "She'd been takin' lessons fr'm a Dutchman down th' sthreet, an' they say she can play as aisy with her hands crossed as she can with wan finger. She's been whalin' away iver since, an' Donahue is dhrinkin' again.

"Ye see th' other night some iv th' la-ads wint over f'r to see whether they cud smash his table in a frindly game iv forty-fives. I don't know what possessed Donahue. He niver asked his frinds into the parlor befure. They used to set in th' dining-room; an', whin Mrs. Donahue coughed at iliven o'clock, they'd toddle out th' side dure with their hats in their hands. But this here night, whether 'twas that Donahue had taken on a dhrink or two too much, or not, he asked thim all in th' front room, where Mrs. Donahue was settin' with Molly. 'I've brought me frinds,' he says, 'f'r to hear Molly take a fall out iv th' music-box,' he says. 'Let me have ye'er hat, Mike,' he says. "Ye'll not feel it whin ye get out,' he says.

"At anny other time Mrs. Donahue'd give him th' marble heart. But they wasn't a man in th' party that had a pianny to his name, an' she knew they'd be trouble whin they wint home an' tould about it. ''Tis a mel-odjious insthrument,' says she. 'I cud sit here be the hour an' listen to Bootoven and Choochooski,' she says.

"'What did thim write?' says Cassidy. 'Chunes," says Donahue, 'chunes. Molly,' he says, 'fetch 'er th' wallop to make th' gintlemen feel good,' he says. 'What'll it be, la-ads?' 'D'ye know "Down be th' Tan-yard Side"?' says Slavin. "No,' says Molly. 'It goes like this,' says Slavin, 'A-ah, din yadden, yooden a-yadden, arrah yadden ay-a' "I din-now it,' says th' girl. "'Tis a low chune, annyhow,' says Mrs. Donahue. 'Mister Slavin ividintly thinks he's at a polis pic-nic,' she says. 'I'll have no come-all-ye's in this house,' she says. 'Molly, give us a few ba-ars fr'm Wagner.' "What Wagner's that?' says Flanagan. 'No wan ye know,' says Donahue; 'he's a German musician.' 'Thim Germans is hot people f'r music,' says Cassidy. 'I knowed wan that cud play th' "Wacht am Rhine" on a pair iv cymbals,' he says. 'Whisht!' says Donahue. 'Give th' girl a chanst.'

"Slavin tol' me about it. He says he niver heered th' like in his born days. He says she fetched th' pianny two or three wallops that made Cassidy jump out iv his chair, an' Cassidy has charge iv th' steam whistle at th' quarry at that. She wint at it as though she had a gredge at it. First 'twas wan hand an' thin th' other, thin both hands, knuckles down; an' it looked, says Slavin, as if she was goin' to leap into th' middle iv it with both feet, whin Donahue jumps up. 'Hol' on!' he says. 'That's not a rented pianny, ye daft girl,' he says. 'Why, pap-pah,' says Molly, 'what d'ye mean?' she says. 'That's Wagner,' she says. "'Tis th' music iv th' future,' she says. 'Yes,' says Donahue, 'but I don't want me hell on earth. I can wait f'r it,' he says, 'with th' kind permission iv Mrs. Donahue,' he says. 'Play us th' "Wicklow Mountaineer,"' he says, 'an' threat th' masheen kindly,' he says. 'She'll play no "Wicklow Mountaineer,"' says Mrs. Donahue. "If ye want to hear that kind iv chune, ye can go down to Finucane's Hall,' she says, 'an' call in Crowley, th' blind piper,' she says. 'Molly,' she says, 'give us wan iv them Choochooski things,' she said. 'They're so ginteel.'

"With that Donahue rose up. 'Come on,' says he. 'This is no place f'r us,' he says. Slavin, with th' politeness iv a man who's getting' even, turns at th' dure. 'I'm sorry I can't remain,' he says. 'I think th' wurruld an' all iv Choochooski,' he says. 'Me brother used to play his chunes,' he says, — me brother Mike, that run th' grip ca-ar,' he says. 'But there's wan thing missin' fro'm Molly's playin', he says. 'And what may that be?' says Mrs. Donahue. 'An ax,' says Slavin, backin' out.

"So Donahue has took to dhrink."

At the Opera

Edward W. Townsend
Chimmie McFadden and Mr. Paul
1902

Giving Mr. Paul his boxing excise de odder day, he says to me, "Chames," he says, "I just has just read, in a great novel called 'On Your Way,' dat de best cure for a strong toist is to get a rap on your coco."

"Not me," I says; "a punch on de conk gives me a toist."

"Dat being de case," he says, "we will put on smaller gloves, and lay love-taps aside for a round or two."

My, my! For de next tree rounds I had de hustle of me life. Mr. Paul isn't quite so smart as me getting in and away, and side-stepping, but he can hit harder, and dat makes an even match of it. Say, someting was doing for fair; when we quits dere was a little washing up to do, and we used up a bit of court-plaster after dat.

I was wondering what was boddering Mr. Paul. Of course I likes a friendly scrap whenever one comes me way, but he only calls for de small gloves when something is on his mind dat scratches.

I tells Duchess about it, and she says, "De American gentleman is *bizarre*," she says.

"Dey arre," says I. "You ought to know; you landed one."

"*C'est vrai*," she says. "But I speak of de odder kind, not de Bowery gent. If something have distress de American gentleman he want de fight — what you say? — *le boxe*. Wit de gentleman of France it is not so. If his heart is trouble he write poetry, or drink absence. Why not?"

"Search me," I says. "I don't know de answer. What's de best way to catch a squirrel?"

"Search me," says she.

"Climb a tree, and make a noise like a nut," I says.

"Dat is of a nonsense! I knows de trouble wit M'sieu Paul," says she.

"Give it a name," says I.

"It is love," she says.

"He must have it hard," I says, feeling of me eye.

"It is a grand passion," says Duchess, looking a tousand miles over me head.

"It's out of sight," I says. "If Mr. Paul has it for keeps, I'll go into training, so dat I can give him all de sympaty he wants."

"Sympaty is not de cure," she says. "Let me put some hot water on your eye. Did he give you a tip?"

"He did," I says. "He give me a couple of seats for de opray."

"*Quel régal!*" says Duchess. "It is 'Faust.' I'll keep your eye in hot water all day, so dat you shall not look of such drollness."

Say, we went all right. Did you ever see dat opray? It's de finest play I ever see out on top de stoige, and has songs in it, too. It makes "Florrie Dorrie" look like bad money. It was wrote by a fren of Duchess. He knows his business. Let me tell you foist about how we broke into de opray teeater.

I puts on me best harness — de dress close Mr. Paul give me — and Duchess! Say, Miss Fannie must give her a trunk key and told her to help herself. From her waistband down she was a dream, a peach! Above dat — well, in de street it was all right, 'cause she wored a big cloak, and it was warm in de Opray House, so she didn't take cold. She took chances, dough. But no more dan de loidies in de boxes. Some of 'em looked like dey was playing peek-a-boo over de edge of a bat-tub. Dey calls it full dress. I calls dat getting gay wit de laugwudge, if I knows de meaning of "full."

Well, when we gets to de teeater dere was a million carriages on Broadway and bote side streets.

"I wish," says Duchess, "we could come in a carriage. Me *toilette* deserves it."

"Dat's easy," I says.

We chases around to de side street where a lot of coachmen I knows was unloading deir folks. I tips de wink to one coachy, he cops me game, we jumps in, and rides around de corner like we'd come a mile. Tiger opens for us proper, I hands out Duchess, tiger and coachy salutes solemn, and we butts into de push. Listen: in de middle of de sidewalk I steps on de toes of Kelly, de B.Y. cop I knows.

"Make way! Me good man," I says to him. "You has two left feet," I says. "Make way!"

I don't tink he has caught up wit his breat yet.

But I was going to tell you about de opray. In de foist act dere is an old gazeaboo who tinks again when he hears some Easter bells, so he sings a song.

Dat's de trouble wit opray; notting doing till somebody has a chance to sing a song. It's like de smokers I goes to in me precinct club. We'll be all ready to see a pair of lightweights do a few rounds, when de announcer says, "Mr. Cully will oblige wit a song." It's to de bad.

Well, a gang outside sings a song, and de gazeaboo says he'll call on his spirit and see if he can't change his luck. Dis brings on a head-liner wit a name I never could tell you in a tousand years. I can't get furder wit it dan "*Mephis*" Duchess says it's a forn woid for de devil. Anyway, he tells de gazeaboo to cheer up; dat he'll give him de time of his life if he'll sign to play ball wit him whenever he's wanted.

"In a minute!" says de gazeaboo. Dey does stunts wit red fire; *Mephis* shows him a picture of a goil what will be his steady; dey sings a song, and *Faust* — dat's de gaze-aboo — is changed to a dude witout leaving de stoige. Say, it's great!

De head-liner goil is named *Maggie*. Not quite dat, but let it go at dat. She wears her hair like de goil in de song from Hackensack, but *Faust* is a dead swell mug for fair. He meets *Maggie* on her way home, and gives her de glad eye. But she is a good goil, and gives him de trun-down.

"What's doing?" says *Faust* to *Mephissy*. "Your red–fire stunts is no good," he says. "You gets gay too suddent," says *Mephissy*. "You has been a back number so long you is not next to de ways of fashionable society," he says. "Dat was not a trun-down for fair; it was de haughty bluff. You led hearts out of turn, and she renigged. We'll play diamonds wit her next, and see does dat suit her hand," says *Mephissy*.

But before *Mephissy* gets to woik a cowboy, named *Siebel*, what has been *Maggie's* steady, fetches a bunch of flowers to *Maggie's* back yard, and leaves 'em dere for her. He sings a song, sure.

Den *Mephissy* comes in, pipes de flowers de lad has left, and says, "Nay, nay! Dat young poisson can't play in dis back yard. Dis will make her forget her *Sieby* and his roses," and he leaves a box of diamonds dere. He was a wood-sawyer, dat mug.

Den *Maggie* comes on. She makes a bluff at spinning, but de only yarn she spun was a song about *Faust*. She says he's de slickest young man she ever see coming down de lane. She finds de flowers, and lets on she's tickled to deat; but when she cops de diamonds — dat's de finish of de flowers! What?

Nobody asks her to, but she obliges wit anodder song while she tries on de sparklers; and den *Faust* and *Mephissy* breaks into de game. *Faust* asks *Maggie* what's de matter wit his being her steady. She can't give him a heart-to-heart talk till *Mephissy* jollies an old lady out of de way. Den, barring a song or two, dey gets along pretty well till *Maggie* tells him it's time for him to chase himself. He chases; but she forgets her manners, peeps tru de blinds, and fetches him back — wit a song.

But de next act is a corker! *Maggie* has a brodder named *Val*, who is going off to de Philippines to get fever or promotion. Before he goes he naturally comes on de stoige wit his regiment to sing a song. Dat was de boss song of all.

Well, Val was a serapper, of course, and seeing *Faust* hanging around, he says to him, "On your way! Don't get gay around dis corner," he says. "To de woods!" *Faust* says he has as much right to travel in dat ward as Val, and from slanging each odder dey pulls deir swords. Listen: *Val* could done him. He could got de decision if de scrap was on de level, but it wasn't. *Mephissy*, seeing *Faust* up against it, pulls his sword, too, and *Val* couldn't stand off de community of interest.

It wasn't a square deal. I told Duchess so, but she pinches me, and tells me to hold me tongue, 'causes *Val* was due on a song.

Sure money! *Val* tells *Maggie* what he tinks of her — and he trun her no bouquets — and she waits for him to sing his song, and falls on him so he couldn't take a encore. Coitain.

Den Duchess jaws me! "You has no more manners," she says, "daun de swells in de boxes. If you must talk," she says, "hire a box."

De last act is in Sing Sing. And dat's no joke, too. *Maggie* is dere, but has lost her good close, her back comb, her mind, and near everyting but her singing voice. Dat's doing business at de old stand. I didn't hear what she was jailed for. *Mephissy* and *Faust* has a pull wit de jailer, and dey calls on *Maggie*, to say dey'll go bail for her if she'll go along wit dem. She says she'd radder stay where she is dan travel in such company. Dey says, "So long; but as we is all in jail togedder, let us, anyway, have a song before we part."

Of course dey had it. It was a lulu, too, but I don't know what it was about, for Duchess was so croisy mad at de folks putting on cloaks and rubbers while de song was going on, she wouldn't tell me a woid.

Say, she had a right not to rag me for talking at de opray. I never peeped but once, and den I whispered.

I didn't know why folks talks at de opray, so I asks Mr. Paul about it.

"Chames," he says, "when de Carnegie Institution at Washington is open for business, I shall make original research into dis matter you mention. Andrew is a good soul to put up de ten millions to let me do it. I shall devote de remaining days of a melancholy life to discover de reason why folks goes to de opray to talk."

"Why don't you ask some woman?" I says. "Dey does most de talking."

"I knows none of dose women, but will consent to meet one for de sum Mr. Carnegie donates. Den, by a short soul-to-soul chat, I hopes to explain," he says, "de phenomenon."

Bill's Tenor and My Bass

Eugene Fields
Single Blessedness and Other Observations, 1922

Bill was short and dapper, while I was thin and tall;
I had flowin' whiskers, but Bill had none at all;
  Clothes would never seem to set so nice on *me* as him, —
Folks used to laugh, and say I was too powerful slim, —
But Bill's clothes fit him like the paper on the wall;
  And we were the sparkin'est beaus in all the place
  When Bill sung tenor and I sung bass.

Cyrus Baker's oldest girl was member of the choir, —
Eyes as black as Kelsey's cat, and cheeks as red as fire!
  She had the best sopranner voice I think I ever heard, —
Sung "Coronation," "Burlington," and "Chiny" like a bird;

Never done better than with Bill a-standin' nigh 'er.
  A-holdin' of her hymn-book so she wouldn't lose the
  place,
  When Bill sung tenor and I sung bass.

Then there was Prudence Hubbard, so cosey-like and
  fat, —
She sung alto, and wore a pee-wee hat;
Beaved her around one winter, and, first thing I knew,
  One evenin' on the portico I up and called her "Prue"!
But, sakes alive! She didn't mind a little thing like that;
  On all the works of Providence she set a cheerful face
  When Bill was singin' tenor and I was singin' bass.

Bill, nevermore we two shall share the fun we used to
  then,
Nor know the comfort and the peace we had together
  when
  We lived in Massachusetts in the good old courtin'
  days.
  And lifted up our voices in psalms and hymns of
  praise.
Oh, how I wisht that I could live them happy times again!
  For life, as we boys knew it, had a sweet, peculiar
  grace
  When you was singin' tenor and I was singin' bass.

The music folks have nowadays ain't what it used to be,
Because there ain't no singers now on earth like Bill and
  me.
  Why, Lemuel Bangs, who used to go to Springfield
  twice a year,
  Admitted that for singin' Bill and me had not a peer
When Bill went soarin' up to A and I dropped down to D!
The old bull-fiddle Beza Dimmitt played warn't in the
  race
  'Longside of Bill's high tenor and my sonorious bass.

Bill moved to Californy in the spring of 54,
And we folks that used to know him never knew him any
  more;

Then Cyrus Baker's oldest girl, she kind o' pined a spell,
And, hankerin' after sympathy, it naturally befell
That she married Deacon Pitkin's boy, who kep' the general store;
And so the years, the changeful years, have rattled on apace.
Since Bill sung tenor and I sung bass.

As I was settin' by the stove this evenin' after tea,
I noticed wife kep' hitchin' close and closer up to me;
And as she patched the gingham frock our gran'child wore to-day,
I heerd her gin a sigh that seemed to come from fur away.
Couldn't help inquirin' what the trouble might be;
"Was thinkin' of the time," says Prue, a-breshin' at her face.
"When Bill sung tenor and you sung bass."

Music

George Ade
Single Blessedness and Other Observations, 1922
Doubleday, Page & Co., NY

You see her for the first time, and somehow she gives you the impression that she has just bitten into a lemon; so you say to yourself, "Probably she plays the piano very well."

Why does perfectly good music have a curdling effect upon its high priests and virginal altar-tenders?

It is made for soothing purposes, so Shakespeare says, yet those who dope themselves too heavily with the rich varieties become temperamental dyspeptics.

Probably it would be awfully hard to room with one who knew too much about music.

The cruel pity lavished by the bridge expert upon the mental defective who fails to comprehend signals is as naught compared with the devastating scorn which the Grieg fanatic visits upon the loyal followers of Irving Berlin.

Men who are not afraid to walk up to a machine gun will run a mile when they see a young woman who has been thoroughly conservatoried.

The light-headed layman whose cerebral corridors are constructed upon the general plan of a cantaloupe always begins to look about and select the nearest exit when the conversation shifts to Grand Opera.

Music is the universal heritage. Somewhere in the flower-dotted fields between Brahms and "The Maiden's Prayer" there is room for all of us to ramble.

The hairy denizens of the studios probably would favour the electric chair for any one who spoke out in defense of any tune that has committed the unpardonable offence of transmitting ecstasy to about ninety per cent of the population.

Popularity need not be a synonym for cheapness and unworthiness. Prunes and sunsets and georgettes and kodaks are popular, but what would our vaunted civilization do without them?

A song which will caress the emotions of several millions of people is of more practical value that the average Congressional enactment. During the period which follows an orgy, what could be more beneficial than a restful diet of mush?

And yet who has the courage to look a tea-drinker straight in the eye and say that he prefers "Mother Machree" by John McCormack to "Tristan and Isolde?"

Speaking as one who has advanced from "Molly Darling" to "La Bohême," it is not to be denied that even the lowly born may learn to handle, and almost assimilate, music which appeals to the head as well as to the heels.

Only a few of us can establish altitude records in the higher realms of music. Be fair in your judgment of those who go up so high that they are no longer visible to the naked eye.

Be comforted by the reflection that all music is good. If jazz could be converted into music it would be all right too.

Because you seek the drugging effects of ragtime, do not contradict those who claim to get an actual kick from the Boston Symphony Orchestra.

Be not ashamed of a sneaking fondness for minstrel songs and the solemn cadences of the old-time hymns. Make no apology for sentimental ballads. Maple-sirup, it is true; but what in the name of Vermont is wrong with maple-sirup?

The monthly issue of "records," the mechanical players, and the invading Lyceum entertainers have carried a lot of real music into the most distant townships. The neighbours are becoming "educated." But they are still deathly afraid of the morbid genius who regards music as a secret cult instead of a general dispensation.

BIBLIOGRAPHY

An Essay Onto Musik, Josh Billings. *Hiz Sayings*. Carleton. 1865.

At the Opera, Edward W. Townsend, from *Chimmie McFadden and Mr. Paul*. 1902.

Bill's Tenor and My Bass, Eugene Fields, *Single Blessedness and Other Observations*. 1922.

Book of American Limericks, Carolyn Wells. 1925.

By Strauss, song from *The Show Is On*, George and Ira Gershwin. 1936.

Don Giovanni, W.A. Mozari. Vienna State Opera. 1958.

English Horn, Laurence McKinney. *People of Note*. 1949. McKinney & Company.

Flute, Laurence McKinney. *People of Note*. 1949. McKinney & Company.

Friendly Advice by Jon Winokur. Sigmund Romberg. Penguin Books. 1994.

Handel's *Sonata in A...Major,* Ian Parrott. Aberystwyth, Wales.

How Rubenstein Played, George Bagby. *The Old Virginia Gentlemen and Other Sketches*. 1850.

How to Understand Music, Robert Benchley. *No Poems Soar (Around the World Backwards, Forewords and Sideways)*. Harper & Bros., New York. 1932.

Jonathan at the Opera, from *Jonathan and His Continent*. Max O'rell and Jack Allyn. 1889.

Just For the Fun of It, Carl Goerch. 1954.

Laughter From the Hip, Leonard Feather and Jack Tracy. *The Lighter Side of Jazz.* Horizon Press, 1963. Reprinted from DeCapo Press, New York, 1979.

Little Patti, Artemus Ward. 1862.

Makin' Whoopee, Gus Kahn. 1886-1941.

More Playboy's Party Jokes, Playboy Magazine. 1965.

Music, from *Single Blessedness and Other Observations*, Doubleday, Page & Company, New York, New York. 1922.

Musical Message, Robert Gordon.

Musical Review Extraordinary, John Phoenix. 1856.

Oboe, Laurence McKinney. *People of Note*. 1949. McKinney & Company.

Philadelphia Record, Edwin H. Schloss. Philadelphia, PA. 1940.

Slavin Contra Wagner, Finley Peter Dunne. *Mr. Dooley in the Heart's of His Countrymen*. 1899.

Song and Story, George Ade. 1931.

Success in Music City, Bo Whaley. *The Official Redneck Handbook.* Rutledge Hill Press, Nashville, TN. 1997.

Sweet Music, Richard Walser, Editor. *Tar Heel Laughter.* University of North Carolina Press, Chapel Hill, NC. 1974.

Symphony of the Southland, Bo Whaley. *The Official Redneck Handbook.* Rutledge Hill Press, Nashville, TN. 1997.

The Conductor, Laurence McKinney. *People of Note.* 1949. McKinney & Company.

The First Piano in a Mining Camp, Sam Davis. 1885. Taken from *Mark Twain's and Other's Library of Wit and Humor.* 1883.

The Harp of a Thousand Strings, William Penn Brannon. From *The Harp of a Thousand Strings, or, Laughter for a Lifetime...*Komically Konkokted by Spavery (SP Avery?). Dick and Fitzgerald Publishers, New York, New York. 1858.

The Jazz Orchestra Menace, Abe Martin.

The Mixed Chorus, Laurence McKinney. *People of Note.* 1949. McKinney & Company.

The Official Redneck Handbook, Bo Whaley. Rutledge Hill Press, Nashville, TN. 1997.

The Third Verse of America, Carl Goerch. Edwards & Broughton Co., Raleigh, NC. 1954.

Tosca, Giacomo Puccini. City Center, New York. 1960.

Tympanum, Laurence McKinney. *People of Note.* 1949. McKinney & Company.

What the Old Timer and Then Some Said to the Feller From Down Country, Allen R. Foley. Stephen Green Press, Brattlesboro, VT.

Whissling, Josh Billings. *Hiz Sayings.* 1865.

CARTOONS:

Booth, George — Stoneybrooke, NY.

Bucella, Martin — Cheektowaga, NY.

Crenshaw, George — Hollister, CA.

Day, Chon — Westerly, RI.

Hawkins, Johnny — Sherwood, MI.

Masters Agency — Hollister, CA.

Pletcher, E. L. — Slidell, LA.

Schwadron, Harley — Ann Arbor, MI.

The Chicago Sun Times — Chicago, IL.

The Saturday Evening Post Society — Indianapolis, IN.

Zanco, M. L. — Waukegan, IL.

Also available from Lincoln-Herndon Press:

*Grandpa's Rib-Ticklers and Knee-Slappers ....$ 8.95
*Josh Billings—America's Phunniest Phellow...$ 7.95
 Davy Crockett—Legendary Frontier Hero ....$ 7.95
 Cowboy Life on the Sidetrack...$ 7.95
 A Treasury of Science Jokes ....$ 9.95
 The Great American Liar—Tall Tales...$ 9.95
 The Cowboy Humor of A.H. Lewis ....$ 9.95
 The Fat Mascot—22 Funny Baseball Stories and More ....$ 7.95
 A Treasury of Farm and Ranch Humor...$10.95
 Mr. Dooley—We Need Him Now! ....$ 8.95
 A Treasury of Military Humor $10.95
 Here's Charley Weaver, Mamma and Mt. Idy..$ 9.95
 A Treasury of Hunting and Fishing Humor $10.95
 A Treasury of Senior Humor $10.95
 A Treasury of Medical Humor $10.95
 A Treasury of Husband and Wife Humor...$10.95
 A Treasury of Religious Humor...$10.95
 A Treasury of Farm Women's Humor $12.95
 A Treasury of Office Humor $10.95
 A Treasury of Cocktail Humor...$10.95
 A Treasury of Business Humor...$12.95
 A Treasury of Mom, Pop & Kids' Humor..$12.95
 The Humorous Musings of a School Principal $12.95
 A Treasury of Police Humor...$12.95
 A Treasury of Veterinary Humor $12.95
 A Treasury of Musical Humor $12.95

*Available in hardback

The humor in these books will delight you, brighten your conversation, make your life more fun, and healthier, because "Laughter is the Best Medicine."

$3.00 shipping and handling for the first book, and an extra 50¢ per additional book.

Order from:
The Lincoln-Herndon Press, Inc.
818 South Dirksen Parkway
Springfield, IL 62703
(217) 522-2732
FAX (217) 544-8738
Visit our website at: www.lincolnherndon.com